WEBER'S ON THE GRILL™

CHICKEN & SIDES

P9-CRQ-039

by Jamie Purviance

Photography by Tim Turner

Author	Jamie Purviance
Managing editor	Marsha Capen
Photographer and photo art direction	Tim Turner
Food stylist	Lynn Gagné
Assistant food stylist	Nina Albazi
Photo assistant	Christy Clow
Digital guru	Takamasa Ota
Indexer	Becky LaBrum
Color imaging and in-house prepress	Weber Creative Services
Contributors	Jessica Bard, Elizabeth Brown, Carolynn Carreño, Katherine Cobbs, April Cooper, Sarah Epstein, Lillian Kang, Kevin Kolman, Janet McCracken, Louisa Neumann, Tripp Rion, Rick Rodgers, Anne Martin Rolke, Cheryl Sternman Rule, Bob and Coleen Simmons, James Temple
Design and production	rabble+rouser, inc. Christina Schroeder, Chief Rouser Marsha Capen, Editorial Director Shum Prats, Creative Director Elaine Chow, Art Director Erick Collier, Interactive Art Director
Weber-Stephen Products Co.	Mike Kempster Sr., Executive Vice President Sherry L. Bale, Director, Public Relations Brooke Jones, Marketing Manager
Round Mountain Media	Susan Maruyama, Consulting Publishing Director
Oxmoor House, Inc.	Jim Childs, Vice President and Publishing Director Fonda Hitchcock, Brand Manager Susan Payne Dobbs, Editorial Director

© 2010 Weber-Stephen Products Co. No part of this book may be reproduced in any form including, but not limited to, storage in a retrieval system or transmission in any form or by any means, electronic, mechanical, photocopied, scanned, downloaded, recorded, or otherwise, without prior written permission. Weber, the kettle configuration, ♟, Sear Station, and the kettle silhouette are registered trademarks; On the Grill and Weber Style are trademarks; all of Weber-Stephen Products Co., 200 East Daniels Road, Palatine, Illinois 60067 USA. All rights reserved.

Tabasco is a registered trademark of McIlhenny Company, Avery Island, Louisiana; Kick'n Chicken is a registered trademark of ACH Food Companies, Inc., Cordova, Tennessee; Parmigiano-Reggiano is a registered certification trademark owned by Consorzio Del Formaggio Parmigiano-Reggiano, Republic of Italy.

10 9 8 7 6 5 4 3 2 1

ISBN-10: 0-376-02035-0
ISBN-13: 978-0-376-02035-2
Library of Congress Control Number: 2009941654

Weber Customer Service: 1.800.446.1071

www.weber.com® • www.sunset.com • www.oxmoorhouse.com • www.rabbleandrouser.com

WEBER'S ON THE GRILL: **CHICKEN & SIDES**

Table of Contents

Early in my cooking career I worked in the hot basement kitchen of a French bistro in San Francisco. When the delivery trucks rolled up in the morning with cases of raw food, I was one of the prep cooks assigned to peeling, chopping, and butchering whatever the chefs upstairs in the air-conditioned exhibition kitchen needed that day. One day I was working slowly on my gazillionth case of whole chickens and the executive chef looked at me disapprovingly, as if to say, "What's up? Pick up the pace, Jamie."

That day I told the chef flatly that I was sick and tired of chicken. I wanted to get my hands on something spectacular like wild abalone or black truffles. He stared me down the way executive chefs are inclined to do and picked up a chicken thigh from my cutting board. He wagged it right in front of my face and said, "This … this can be as spectacular as you make it."

"What do you mean?" I replied. "It's just chicken."

He grimaced and darted upstairs to the exhibition kitchen. Later that day he returned with a plate of herb-crusted chicken still warm and crispy from the grill. "Taste this," he said.

As I bit through crackling skin, the tender meat below released flavors of white wine, fresh thyme, shallots, and garlic. The juicy meat had the savory depth and richness of chicken soup plus the smokiness of the grill's charcoal embers.

"That's amazing," I admitted. "How did you make that?"

"A grandmother from Provence taught me that. You just took a bite out of the history of French cuisine. Are you really going to tell me that's boring?"

I had nothing to say. My complaint about chicken was now obviously at odds with centuries of brilliant cooking.

That lesson stood with me as I was writing this book. As I worked on the recipes here, I drew heavily from the cooking traditions all over the world and I was inspired by how well grilled chicken lends itself to so many international options, including salads, gyros, stews, kabobs, tacos, burgers, wraps, and panini. And that's just the beginning.

Like a lot of home cooks, I appreciate fast and fabulous recipes that I can grill when time is short. If that's you, too, I want to steer you toward the Grilled Chicken Tacos with Lime-Cilantro Slaw (page 85), the Chicken Cobb Salad and Lemon-Mustard Dressing (page 72), and the Lemon-Dill Chicken Wraps with Grated Carrots (page 82). For busy families trying to eat well on busy weeknights, these work out great.

On occasion I like to be a little more lavish and improvisational, so I've also included recipes like Prosciutto-Wrapped Chicken with Fig-Balsamic Glaze (page 96), Turkish Chicken Kabobs with Red Pepper and Walnut Sauce (page 102), and Barbecued Chicken Pizza with Smoked Mozzarella (page 88). As you will see, it's really quite simple to jazz up chicken on the grill; the flavors play well with almost anything. The key is learning the proper techniques for each particular piece of chicken and using the right level of heat for the right length of time. All that is covered in the following pages.

The next time you are at the supermarket staring into the refrigerated shelves of pale chicken, I hope you will look past what appears to be bland and remember what you have in this book. It's a full spectrum of honest, passionate grilling reflecting the best of what people all over the world do with grilled chicken. What's boring about that? Enough said. Let's grill.

Jamie Purviance

WHAT TO LOOK FOR IN CHICKEN

Chicken is chicken, right? Not exactly. Most supermarkets carry big national brands, or sometimes supermarkets put their own brands on these mass-produced birds raised in cages. They are low in fat, they cook quickly, and they are pretty tender; however, their flavor is pretty darn bland. Fortunately the grill provides just what they need. With a little oil, some seasonings, and maybe a sauce, they are very good on the grill.

Today we are seeing more premium chickens available, and usually they are worth their higher price, though not always. Typically these chickens are from old-fashioned breeds known more for their flavor than their plump breasts and perfectly even shape. Often called "free-range" chickens, they have access to the outdoors, or at least the freedom to wander indoors. The exercise contributes to firmer, more flavorful meat. Check them out. Any chickens you buy should have skins that fit their bodies well, not spotty or shriveled or too far overlapping. The color of the skin says little about quality, but the smell of a chicken will tell you everything you need to know about freshness. If it smells funny, don't buy it.

By law, the USDA insists that every chicken be chilled to at least 40°F within 4 hours of being slaughtered. Typically producers submerge their chickens in chlorinated ice water, which works quickly, but often the process means that the chickens absorb some water. Another process, which is not as common in the United States, involves spraying the chickens with chlorinated water and then sending them though long tunnels filled with cold air. The air-chilled chickens absorb less water, which is good. Who wants to pay extra for ice water?

Some chickens, even when they have been properly chilled, carry bacteria like salmonella. There is no sense in rinsing raw chickens prior to cooking. That would only raise the chances of spreading bacteria around your kitchen. Simply cook your chickens properly, and all the dangerous bacteria will be killed.

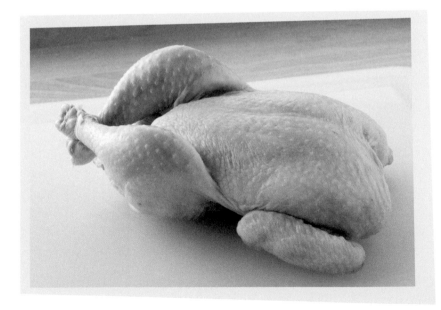

To check the doneness of a bone-in chicken thigh, pull one of the thickest ones from the grill and cut into the underside. If the color of the meat near the bone is still pink, put it back on the grill until it is fully cooked.

WHAT YOU NEED TO KNOW

BONELESS, SKINLESS BREASTS AND THIGHS. Boneless pieces are usually best grilled over direct medium heat for 8 to 12 minutes. For maximum flavor, leave them alone as much as possible. The longer they stay in place on the hot grate, the deeper the flavors will be, so try to turn them just once or twice.

BONE-IN BREASTS. With these, you are wise to consider a strategy that involves both direct and indirect medium heat. Start them over direct heat until golden brown on both sides, which takes 6 to 10 minutes. At this point, if you left the breasts over direct heat much longer, they would burn. So move the breasts over indirect heat and let them finish cooking there. Typically that takes about 20 minutes.

One good alternative approach for bone-in breasts is to start them over indirect medium heat, with the bone side down, and let them cook there for 30 to 45 minutes. This avoids almost any chance of flare-ups, but the skin is less likely to turn golden brown and crispy, so during the final 5 minutes or so of cooking, you might want to move them over direct heat, with the skin side down.

BONE-IN LEGS. Treat bone-in thighs, drumsticks, and whole legs in ways similar to bone-in breasts. The dark meat will just take longer to cook. So if you brown them first over direct medium heat for 6 to 10 minutes, turning them once, and then finish them over indirect medium heat, that finishing time will be 25 to 35 minutes. Cooking them entirely over indirect medium heat would take 40 to 50 minutes.

WHOLE BIRDS. Whole chickens are difficult to brown evenly over direct heat and there's really no need to even try. The skin will brown beautifully if you simply roast the bird over indirect medium heat for 1¼ to 1½ hours. The wing tips have almost no meat and they tend to burn, so you may want to remove them at the joint with a sharp knife or poultry shears prior to grilling.

NO MATTER WHAT. Regardless of the type of chicken you are grilling, brush the surfaces lightly with oil and season them generously. Remember that some of the seasoning is likely to fall off during cooking. And always keep the lid closed as much as possible. This will prevent flare-ups, speed up the cooking time, and capture the smokiness of the grill.

TRUSSING THE CHICKEN

The wing tips have almost no meat and they tend to burn, so remove them at the joint with poultry shears.

Slide a 4-foot length of butcher's twine under the legs and back.

Lift both ends of the twine and cross them between the legs. Then run one end under one drumstick.

Run the other end under the other drumstick and pull both ends to draw the drumsticks together.

Bring the twine along both sides of the chicken so that it holds the legs and wings against the body.

Tie a knot in the ends between the neck and the top of the breast. If necessary, push the breast down a little to expose more of the neck.

POSITIONING THE CHICKEN ON THE ROTISSERIE SPIT

Position one set of fork prongs on the far end of the spit and slide the spit into the opening between the neck and the knotted twine, through the chicken, and out the other side, just underneath the drumsticks.

Slide the other set of fork prongs on the spit and drive the prongs into the back of the chicken.

Make sure the chicken is centered on the spit before tightening the fork prongs into place.

ADAPTING RECIPES TO THE ROTISSERIE

Almost any recipe that calls for indirect heat does really well on the rotisserie. As long as the meat can be evenly balanced on the spit, it's a prime candidate for the rotisserie.

By the same token, if your grill doesn't have a rotisserie, you can still cook any recipe that calls for one. Just put the meat right on the cooking grate over indirect heat, with the fire on opposite sides of the food. The cooking time and temperature will be almost exactly the same.

Grilling Fundamentals

GRILLING KNOW-HOW

THE DIFFERENCE BETWEEN DIRECT AND INDIRECT COOKING

With direct heat, the fire is right below the food. With indirect heat, the fire is off to one side of the grill, or on both sides of the grill, and the food sits over the unlit part.

Direct heat works great for small, tender pieces of food that cook quickly, including boneless chicken breasts and thighs. It sears the surfaces of these foods, developing delicious flavors and textures, while cooking the meat all the way to the center. It is also the right heat to use for browning bone-in pieces before finishing them over indirect heat.

Indirect heat works more slowly on the food, allowing the inside of chicken to cook at about the same rate as the outside. So it's the best choice for whole chickens and any bone-in pieces that need more than 30 minutes of grilling time. Also use this kind of heat when you are grilling smoked chicken.

SETTING UP YOUR CHARCOAL GRILL FOR DIRECT AND INDIRECT COOKING

First things first. You'll need fuel, and the simplest way to measure the right amount of fuel for your charcoal grill is to use a chimney starter. Use it like a measuring cup for charcoal. Fill it to the rim with briquettes or lump charcoal, and burn them until they are lightly covered with ash.

Spread the coals in a tightly packed, single layer across one-half to two-thirds of the charcoal grate. Put the cooking grate in place, close the lid, and let the coals burn down to the desired heat. Leave all the vents open. This basic configuration is called a two-zone fire because you have one zone of direct heat and one zone of indirect heat. It's the setup you'll use most often. The temperature of a two-zone fire can be high, medium, or low, depending on how much charcoal is burning and how long it has been burning. Remember, charcoal loses heat over time.

few minutes and then reconnect the hose. Try lighting the grill again. If you still smell gas, shut the grill down and call Weber Customer Service.

You can switch from direct to indirect heat almost immediately. Just turn off one or more of the burners and place the food over an unlit burner. If your grill has just two burners, turn off the one toward the back of the grill. If your grill has more than two burners, turn off the one(s) in the middle of the grill. The burners that are left on can be set to high, medium, or low heat, as desired. Whenever the food is over an unlit burner and the lid is closed, you're grilling over indirect heat.

SETTING UP YOUR GAS GRILL FOR DIRECT AND INDIRECT COOKING

There's nothing complicated about lighting a gas grill. However, gas grill operation does vary, so be sure to consult the owner's manual that came with your grill. To light a Weber® gas grill, first open the lid so unlit gas fumes don't collect in the cooking box. Next, slowly open the valve on your propane tank (or natural gas line) all the way and wait a minute for the gas to travel through the gas line. Then turn on the burners, setting them all to high. Close the lid and preheat the grill for 10 to 15 minutes. Then simply leave all the burners on and adjust them for the heat level you want.

If you smell gas, turn off all the burners. Close the valve on your propane tank (or natural gas line) and disconnect the hose. Wait a

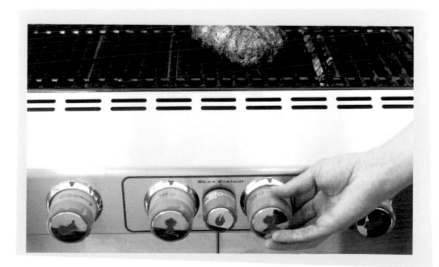

Grilling Fundamentals

ESSENTIAL TOOLS FOR THE GRILLER

TONGS

Definitely the hardest working tool of all. You will need three pairs: one for raw food, one for cooked food, and one for arranging charcoal.

GRILL PAN

Here's a great tool for grilling small foods that might otherwise fall through the cooking grate, like mushrooms and cherry tomatoes. Be sure to preheat the pan before the food goes on.

CHIMNEY STARTER

This is the simplest tool for starting lump charcoal or briquettes faster and more evenly than you could with lighter fluid. Look for one with a capacity of at least 5 quarts.

GRILL BRUSH

Spring for a solid, long-handled model with stainless steel bristles. Use it to clean off the cooking grates before you grill and during grilling.

INSTANT-READ THERMOMETER

Use this little gadget to check the doneness of a whole chicken. Simply insert the probe in the thickest part of the thigh and avoid touching the bone, which could lead to a false reading (bones conduct heat).

SHEET PAN

A baking sheet like this one does a lot more than bake. It is a great portable work surface for oiling and seasoning foods, and there's nothing better to use as a landing pad for chicken coming off the grill.

BARBECUE MITTS

Protect your hands and forearms when managing a charcoal fire or reaching toward the back of a hot grill.

SPATULA

Look for a long-handled spatula designed with a bent (offset) neck so that the blade is set lower than the handle. It's a good alternative to tongs for flipping chicken and other foods.

BASTING BRUSH

A good brush is always helpful for oiling your chicken and applying your glazes and sauces. Today's brushes with stainless steel handles and silicon bristles can go right into the dishwasher.

TIMER

As the old saying goes, timing is everything ... that and temperature, because every great chicken recipe depends on the right combination of timing and temperature.

14

WHOLE BIRDS

16 Brined and Roasted Chicken with Oregano and Tarragon
18 Whole Roasted Chicken with Fennel Salt
19 Beer Can Chicken Seasoned with Garlic, Lemon, and Herbs
20 Moroccan-Spiced Rotisserie Chicken
22 Rosemary Chicken under Bricks with Grilled Lemons
24 Cornish Hens with Orange-Curry Glaze

BONE-IN CHICKEN PIECES

26 Picnic Chicken Provençal with White Bean Salad
27 Pulled Chicken Sandwiches with Smoky Barbecue Sauce
28 Barbecued Chicken Marinated in Lemon, Garlic, and Oyster Sauce
30 Tandoori Chicken Marinated in Yogurt and Indian Spices
31 Garlic Chicken with Rosemary and Lemon
32 Barbecued Chicken with Bourbon-Bacon Sauce
34 Grilled Chicken Adobo with Vinegar and Soy Sauce
35 Skillet-Roasted Chicken with Fresh Thyme and Garlic Potatoes
36 Ginger-Marinated Drumsticks with Coconut Milk and Honey
38 Ancho Chile Chicken Thighs with Tomato Chutney
40 Spicy Chicken Thighs with Citrus-Fennel Relish
41 Moroccan Chicken Thighs Marinated in Red Pepper Paste
42 Thighs and Drumsticks with Root Beer Barbecue Sauce
43 Oak-Smoked Thighs with Hoisin Glaze
44 Chicken Breasts with Lime Crema
46 Chicken Breasts with Smoked Paprika Butter
48 Cajun Chicken Breasts with Grilled Corn and Black-Eyed Pea Salsa
49 Chinese Chicken Wings with Honey and Soy Glaze
50 Hot Wings with Blue Cheese Dressing

GROUND CHICKEN

52 Blue Cheese Chicken Patty Melts with Grilled Onions
54 Southwestern Green Chile Chicken Cheeseburgers
55 Chicken Burgers with Grilled Mushrooms and Rosemary Aioli

BONELESS CHICKEN THIGHS

56 Chicken Thighs Smothered in Corn and Bacon Relish
57 Lemon Chicken and Mint Risotto with Green Peas
58 Smoked Chicken Chili with Corn and Beans
60 Indian Chicken Skewers with Fresh Cilantro Puree
62 Chicken Tacos with Goat Cheese and Roasted Tomato-Garlic Salsa

BONELESS CHICKEN BREASTS

64 Mojito Chicken Breasts
65 Chicken Breasts Drizzled with Orange-Ginger Sauce
66 Grilled Chicken Panzanella with Basil Vinaigrette
68 Chicken and Apple Salad with Cheddar Cheese and Cashews
70 Grilled Chicken Salad Niçoise with Sherry Vinaigrette
71 Chicken Souvlaki with Minty Feta Dressing
72 Chicken Cobb Salad and Lemon-Mustard Dressing
74 Vietnamese Chicken Salad with Lime and Sesame Dressing
75 Farfalle Salad with Grilled Chicken and Summer Vegetables
76 Malaysian Chicken Salad with Cucumbers, Carrots, and Peanut Dressing
78 Honey-Mustard Chicken Sandwiches with Avocado and Arugula
79 Chicken Sandwiches with Pickled Peppers and Creamy Lemon Spread
80 Chicken Cordon Bleu Panini with Ham and Swiss Cheese
82 Lemon-Dill Chicken Wraps with Grated Carrots
84 Paprika Chicken with Romesco Sauce
85 Grilled Chicken Tacos with Lime-Cilantro Slaw
86 Mexican Chicken Bowl with Rice, Beans, and Queso Fresco
88 Barbecued Chicken Pizza with Smoked Mozzarella
89 Kick'n Chicken Breasts with Yogurt-Cucumber Sauce
90 Cumin-Coriander Chicken Breasts with Pumpkin Seed Pesto
91 Marinated Chicken Breasts with Tangerine Salsa
92 Chile-Rubbed Chicken with Jicama, Avocado, and Orange Salsa
94 Chicken Saltimbocca in White Wine-Butter Sauce
96 Prosciutto-Wrapped Chicken with Fig-Balsamic Glaze
98 Chicken Skewers Marinated in Basil and Sun-Dried Tomatoes
99 Chicken, Onion, and Tomato Skewers with Creamy Avocado Sauce
100 Chicken and Peach Kabobs with Blackberry Sauce
102 Turkish Chicken Kabobs with Red Pepper and Walnut Sauce
104 Marinated Chicken Spiedini with Rosemary and Garlic
105 Chicken Tender Skewers Marinated in Green Tea and Ginger
106 Chicken Gyros with Tomato Tzatziki
108 Parmesan-Breaded Chicken with Lemon Aioli
109 Chicken Tender Salad with Melon and Mint

BRINED AND ROASTED CHICKEN
WITH OREGANO AND TARRAGON

PREP TIME: 15 minutes
BRINING TIME: 6 to 8 hours
GRILLING TIME: 1¼ to 1½ hours
SPECIAL EQUIPMENT: butcher's twine,
instant-read thermometer

Brine

- 1 quart water
- ½ cup kosher salt
  Juice of 2 lemons
- 2 tablespoons dried oregano
- 2 tablespoons dried tarragon
- 1 tablespoon granulated garlic
- 2 teaspoons ground black pepper

- 12 cups ice cubes

- 1 whole chicken, 4 to 5 pounds, giblets and any excess fat removed
- 1 tablespoon extra-virgin olive oil

1. In a large pot over medium heat, combine the brine ingredients. Bring to a simmer and stir to dissolve the salt. Add the ice to the pot. Let the liquid cool to room temperature.

2. Submerge the chicken in the brine, with the breast facing down. Refrigerate the chicken in the pot for 6 to 8 hours.

3. Prepare the grill for indirect cooking over medium heat (about 400°F).

4. Remove the chicken from the brine. Discard the brine. Pat the chicken dry with paper towels. Lightly coat the outside of the chicken with the oil. Truss the chicken with butcher's twine (see page 8).

5. Brush the cooking grates clean. Grill the chicken, breast side up, over *indirect medium heat*, with the lid closed, until the juices run clear and the internal temperature reaches 170°F in the thickest part of the thigh (not touching the bone), 1¼ to 1½ hours, rotating the chicken as needed for even cooking and browning. Remove from the grill and let rest for 5 to 10 minutes (the internal temperature will rise 5 to 10 degrees during this time). Cut into serving pieces and serve warm.

SERVES: 4

WHOLE ROASTED CHICKEN
WITH FENNEL SALT

PREP TIME: 20 minutes
GRILL TIME: 1¼ to 1½ hours
SPECIAL EQUIPMENT: spice mill, butcher's twine, instant-read thermometer

Paste

- 2 tablespoons whole fennel seed
- 2 teaspoons kosher salt
- 1 tablespoon extra-virgin olive oil

Dressing

- ⅓ cup extra-virgin olive oil
- 1 teaspoon finely grated orange zest
- 2 tablespoons fresh orange juice
- 1 tablespoon white wine vinegar
- 1 tablespoon minced shallot
- 1 teaspoon reserved fennel salt

- 1 whole chicken, 4 to 5 pounds, giblets and any excess fat removed
- ½ small orange, quartered
- 1 medium shallot, peeled and quartered

1. Put the fennel seed and salt in a spice mill and process until finely ground. Set aside 1 teaspoon of the fennel salt for the dressing. In a small bowl mix the oil with the remaining fennel salt.

2. In a small glass or stainless steel bowl, whisk the dressing ingredients until emulsified.

3. Prepare the grill for indirect cooking over medium heat (about 400°F).

4. Starting at the neck end of the chicken, work your fingertips gently under the skin and over the meat. Use just one finger to reach down each drumstick and along the thigh meat. Rub 2 teaspoons of the paste under the skin onto the breast meat and as much as you can reach on the drumsticks and thighs. Rub the cavity with ½ teaspoon of the paste, and then stuff the cavity with the orange and shallot. Rub the remaining paste all over the chicken. Truss the chicken legs with butcher's twine. Tuck the tips of the wings behind the chicken's back.

5. Brush the cooking grates clean. Grill the chicken, breast side up, over **_indirect medium heat_**, with the lid closed, until the juices run clear and the internal temperature reaches 170°F in the thickest part of the thigh (not touching the bone), 1¼ to 1½ hours. When fully cooked, transfer the chicken to a cutting board and let rest for 5 to 10 minutes (the internal temperature will rise 5 to 10 degrees during this time). Cut the chicken into serving pieces. Whisk the dressing again. Serve the chicken warm with some dressing drizzled on top.

SERVES: 4

18

BEER CAN CHICKEN
SEASONED WITH GARLIC, LEMON, AND HERBS

PREP TIME: 10 minutes
GRILLING TIME: 1¼ to 1½ hours
SPECIAL EQUIPMENT: instant-read thermometer

1 whole chicken, 4 to 5 pounds, giblets and any excess fat removed
2 tablespoons vegetable oil
2 tablespoons Weber® Beer Can Chicken Seasoning
1 can (12 ounces) beer, at room temperature

1. Prepare the grill for indirect cooking over medium heat (about 400°F).

2. Lightly coat the chicken all over with the oil and season evenly with the seasoning. Tuck the tips of the wings behind the chicken's back.

3. Open the beer can and pour out (or drink) about half the beer. Using a can opener, make two more holes in the top of the can. Place the can on a solid surface. Plunk the chicken cavity over the can.

4. Transfer the chicken-on-a-can to the grill, balancing the chicken with its two legs and the can, like a tripod. Grill the chicken over *indirect medium heat*, with the lid closed, until the juices run clear and the internal temperature reaches 170°F in the thickest part of the thigh (not touching the bone), 1¼ to 1½ hours. Carefully remove the chicken-on-a-can from the grill (do not spill the contents of the beer can, as it will be very hot!). Let the chicken rest for 5 to 10 minutes (the internal temperature will rise 5 to 10 degrees during this time) before lifting it from the can and cutting it into serving pieces. Serve warm.

SERVES: 4

MOROCCAN-SPICED ROTISSERIE CHICKEN

PREP TIME: 25 minutes
GRILLING TIME: 1¼ to 1½ hours
SPECIAL EQUIPMENT: butcher's twine, rotisserie, large disposable foil pan, instant-read thermometer

Paste

- 2 tablespoons fresh lemon juice
- 2 tablespoons extra-virgin olive oil
- 1½ teaspoons ground cinnamon
- 1 teaspoon paprika
- 1 teaspoon ground ginger
- 1 teaspoon ground turmeric
- 1 teaspoon ground coriander
- 1 teaspoon kosher salt
- ¾ teaspoon ground cardamom
- ½ teaspoon ground cumin
- ½ teaspoon ground black pepper
- ¼ teaspoon ground nutmeg
- ¼ teaspoon ground allspice

- 1 whole chicken, 4 to 5 pounds, giblets and any excess fat removed
- 1 lemon, cut into 4 wedges
- 4 large mint sprigs

1. In a small bowl combine the paste ingredients.

2. Prepare the grill for indirect cooking over medium heat (about 400°F).

3. Starting at the neck end of the chicken, work your fingertips gently under the skin and over the meat. Try not to tear the skin. Use just one finger to reach down each drumstick and along the thigh meat. Spread some of the paste under the skin and onto the flesh of the chicken. Smear 1 tablespoon of the paste inside the cavity of the chicken, and then stuff with the lemon and mint. Coat the outside of the chicken with the remaining paste. Truss the chicken with butcher's twine (see page 8).

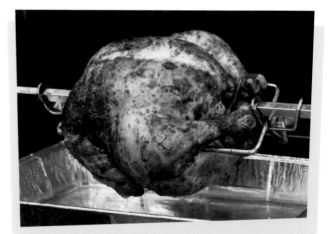

The slow turning of a chicken on a rotisserie browns the skin beautifully while the juices flow evenly throughout the meat. The pan underneath captures any grease, making cleanup simple.

20

4. Secure the chicken in the middle of the rotisserie spit (see page 9), put the spit in place, and turn on the motor. Place a large disposable foil pan under the chicken to catch any drippings, and pour about 1 cup of warm water into the pan. Grill the chicken over **indirect medium heat**, with the lid closed, until the juices run clear and the internal temperature reaches 170°F in the thickest part of the thigh (not touching the bone), 1¼ to 1½ hours.

5. When the chicken is fully cooked, turn off the rotisserie motor and, wearing barbecue mitts, carefully remove the spit from the grill. Tilt the chicken upright over the foil pan so that the liquid that has accumulated in the chicken's cavity pours into the pan. Slide the chicken from the spit onto a cutting board. Let rest for 5 to 10 minutes (the internal temperature will rise 5 to 10 degrees during this time). Cut the chicken into serving pieces and serve warm.

SERVES: 4

ROSEMARY CHICKEN UNDER BRICKS
WITH GRILLED LEMONS

PREP TIME: 20 minutes
MARINATING TIME: 2 to 4 hours
GRILLING TIME: about 1 hour
SPECIAL EQUIPMENT: poultry shears; sheet pan and 2 foil-wrapped bricks or cast-iron skillet; instant-read thermometer

Marinade

- ¼ cup extra-virgin olive oil
- ¼ cup fresh lemon juice
- 1 tablespoon minced fresh rosemary leaves
- 2 teaspoons kosher salt
- 3 garlic cloves, minced

- 1 whole chicken, 4 to 5 pounds, giblets and any excess fat removed

- 2 lemons, halved
  Extra-virgin olive oil

1. Whisk the marinade ingredients in a 13x9-inch glass baking dish.

2. Place the chicken, breast side down, on a cutting board. Using poultry shears, cut from the neck to the tail end, along either side of the backbone, to remove it.

3. Once the backbone is out, you'll be able to see the interior of the chicken. Make a small slit in the cartilage at the bottom end of the breastbone. Then, placing both hands on the rib cage, crack the chicken open like a book. Run your fingers along either side of the cartilage in between the breast to loosen it from the flesh. Grab the bone and pull up on it to remove it along with the attached cartilage. The chicken should now lie flat.

4. Place the chicken in the dish and turn to coat it evenly with the marinade. Cover with plastic wrap and refrigerate for 2 to 4 hours, turning occasionally.

5. Prepare the grill for direct cooking over medium-low heat (about 350°F).

6. Brush the cooking grates clean. Place the chicken, bone side down, over ***direct medium-low heat***. Place the sheet pan on top of the chicken and weight it down with 2 bricks wrapped in foil (or use a cast-iron skillet). Close the lid and cook for 20 to 30 minutes. Wearing barbecue mitts, remove the weight, turn the chicken over, replace the weight, close the lid, and cook until the juices run clear and the internal temperature reaches 170°F in the thickest part of the thigh (not touching the bone), 20 to 30 minutes. Remove from the grill and let rest for 3 to 5 minutes (the internal temperature will rise 5 to 10 degrees during this time).

7. Brush the cut sides of the lemons with oil and grill over ***direct medium-low heat*** until well charred and caramelized, about 5 minutes. Cut the chicken into serving pieces, squeeze the lemons over the chicken, and serve warm.

SERVES: 4

CORNISH HENS
WITH ORANGE-CURRY GLAZE

PREP TIME: 30 minutes
GRILLING TIME: 28 to 47 minutes
SPECIAL EQUIPMENT: poultry shears,
instant-read thermometer

Rub

- 2 teaspoons curry powder
- 1½ teaspoons kosher salt
- ½ teaspoon ground black pepper

- 2 whole Cornish hens, 1½ to 2 pounds each,
  giblets removed
  Extra-virgin olive oil

Glaze

- ½ cup fresh orange juice
- ¼ cup orange marmalade
- 2 tablespoons Scotch whiskey
- 1 tablespoon cider vinegar
- ½ teaspoon kosher salt
- ¼ teaspoon curry powder
- ¼ teaspoon ground black pepper

- 1 tablespoon unsalted butter

1. Prepare the grill for direct and indirect cooking over high heat (450° to 550°F).

2. In a small bowl mix the rub ingredients.

3. Using poultry shears, cut along both sides of each backbone and discard them. Turn the hens over, with the skin side facing up, and press with the palms of both hands to crack the rib bones and flatten the hens.

4. Lightly coat the skin of each hen with oil and season evenly with the rub. Set aside while making the glaze.

5. In a small saucepan combine the glaze ingredients and bring to a boil over high heat. Lower the heat and simmer, stirring occasionally, until the glaze begins to thicken, 5 to 7 minutes. Whisk in the butter, remove from the heat, and set aside.

6. Brush the cooking grates clean. Grill the hens, skin side down, over ***direct high heat***, with the lid closed, until the skin is golden brown, 4 to 6 minutes. Being careful not to tear the skin, turn the hens over and grill them until lightly charred, 4 to 6 minutes.

7. Move the hens over ***indirect high heat*** and cook, skin side up, with the lid closed, for 15 to 20 minutes. Brush the skin with a thin layer of the glaze, using just enough so it doesn't drip into the grill. Continue to cook until the juices run clear and the internal temperature reaches 170°F in the thickest part of the thigh (not touching the bone), 5 to 15 minutes, brushing every 5 minutes with the glaze. Keep the lid closed as much as possible during grilling.

8. Transfer the hens to a cutting board. Brush with the glaze and let rest for about 5 minutes (the internal temperature will rise 5 to 10 degrees during this time). Cut each hen in half lengthwise along the breastbone. Serve warm with additional glaze on the side, if desired.

SERVES: 2 to 4

PICNIC CHICKEN PROVENÇAL
WITH WHITE BEAN SALAD

PREP TIME: 30 minutes
MARINATING TIME: 2 to 4 hours
GRILLING TIME: 30 to 50 minutes

Marinade
- 1 small yellow onion, roughly chopped
- ½ cup loosely packed fresh Italian parsley leaves and tender stems
- ¼ cup fresh rosemary leaves
- 4 large garlic cloves
- 2 tablespoons Dijon mustard
- 2 tablespoons tomato paste
- 2 teaspoons kosher salt
- ½ teaspoon ground black pepper
- ½ cup dry white wine
- ¼ cup extra-virgin olive oil

- 1 whole chicken, 4 to 5 pounds

Dressing
- ¼ cup extra-virgin olive oil
- 2 tablespoons red wine vinegar
- 1 teaspoon minced garlic
- ½ teaspoon kosher salt
- ¼ teaspoon ground black pepper

Salad
- 2 cans (15 ounces each) cannellini beans, rinsed
- 1 cup finely chopped cherry tomatoes
- ½ cup sliced green olives
- ⅓ cup roughly chopped fresh Italian parsley leaves

1. In a food processor or blender, process the marinade ingredients, except the wine and oil, until finely chopped. Then add the wine and oil and process until fairly smooth. Pour the marinade into a large glass or stainless steel bowl.

2. Cut the chicken into eight pieces: two breast pieces, two thigh pieces, two drumsticks, and two wings. Add the chicken pieces to the bowl with the marinade and turn to coat evenly. Cover and refrigerate for 2 to 4 hours.

3. In a large bowl whisk the dressing ingredients. Add the salad ingredients and stir gently to combine. Set aside at room temperature until ready to serve.

4. Prepare the grill for direct and indirect cooking over medium heat (350° to 450°F).

5. Remove the chicken pieces from the bowl and discard the marinade. Brush the cooking grates clean. Grill the chicken, skin side down first, over **indirect medium heat**, with the lid closed, until the juices run clear and the meat is opaque all the way to the bone, turning two or three times. The breasts and wings will take 30 to 40 minutes and the thighs and drumsticks will take 40 to 50 minutes. During the last 10 minutes of grilling time, move the chicken over **direct medium heat** until well browned all over, turning once. Remove from the grill and let rest for 3 to 5 minutes.

6. Place the salad in a wide, shallow bowl and arrange the chicken pieces on top.

SERVES: 4 to 6

PULLED CHICKEN SANDWICHES
WITH SMOKY BARBECUE SAUCE

PREP TIME: 20 minutes, plus about 20 minutes for the sauce
GRILLING TIME: 30 to 50 minutes

Rub
1 tablespoon smoked paprika
1 teaspoon granulated garlic
1 teaspoon granulated onion
1 teaspoon dried oregano
1 teaspoon dried thyme
1 teaspoon kosher salt
¼ teaspoon ground cayenne pepper

1 whole chicken, 4 to 5 pounds
 Extra-virgin olive oil

Sauce
1 cup ketchup
1 cup beer
¼ cup chicken broth
1 tablespoon smoked paprika
1 tablespoon cider vinegar
1 tablespoon unsalted butter
½ teaspoon granulated onion
⅛ teaspoon granulated garlic

4–6 French or kaiser rolls, split

1. Prepare the grill for indirect cooking over medium heat (350° to 450°F).

2. In a small bowl mix the rub ingredients.

3. Cut the chicken into six pieces: two breast pieces, two thigh pieces, and two drumsticks. Reserve the back and wings for another use. Remove and discard the skin. Lightly coat the chicken pieces all over with oil and season evenly with the rub.

4. Brush the cooking grates clean. Grill the chicken, with the meatier sides facing down first, over *indirect medium heat*, with the lid closed as much as possible, until the juices run clear and the meat is opaque all the way to the bone, turning two or three times. The breasts will take 30 to 40 minutes and the thighs and drumsticks will take 40 to 50 minutes. Remove from the grill and let rest while you make the sauce.

5. In a small saucepan over medium-high heat, whisk the sauce ingredients. Bring to a boil and then reduce the heat and simmer for about 15 minutes, stirring frequently, or until the sauce darkens slightly and begins to thicken.

6. Pull or shred the chicken with two forks. Put the chicken in a large bowl and add about ¾ cup of the sauce; mix to coat evenly. Place approximately ¾ cup of chicken on each roll and serve with extra sauce on the side. Serving suggestion: Cajun Corn with Louisiana Butter (for recipe, see page 122).

SERVES: 4 to 6

BARBECUED CHICKEN
MARINATED IN LEMON, GARLIC, AND OYSTER SAUCE

PREP TIME: 15 minutes
MARINATING TIME: 6 to 12 hours
GRILLING TIME: 30 to 50 minutes

Marinade
- ⅔ cup fresh lemon juice
- ½ cup oyster sauce
- 2 tablespoons hot chili-garlic sauce, such as Sriracha
- 1 tablespoon minced fresh ginger

2 whole chickens, 4 to 5 pounds each

The key to this marinade is to balance the rich and salty characteristics of dark oyster sauce with the spiciness of hot chili-garlic sauce and the unique kick of fresh ginger. Lemon juice bridges all the flavors together.

1. In a large glass or stainless steel bowl, whisk the marinade ingredients.

2. Cut each chicken into eight pieces: two breast pieces, two thighs, two drumsticks, and two wings. Remove and discard the wing tips. Add the chicken to the marinade and turn to coat evenly. Cover and refrigerate for 6 to 12 hours, turning occasionally.

3. Prepare the grill for direct and indirect cooking over medium heat (350° to 450°F).

4. Remove the chicken from the bowl and discard the marinade. Brush the cooking grates clean. Grill the chicken pieces, skin side down, over *indirect medium heat*, with the lid closed, until the juices run clear and the meat is opaque all the way to the bone. The breasts and wings will take 30 to 40 minutes and the thighs and drumsticks will take 40 to 50 minutes. During the last 5 minutes of grilling time, move the chicken over *direct medium heat* and cook until well browned all over, turning once. Remove from the grill and let rest for 3 to 5 minutes. Serve warm.

SERVES: 6 to 8

TANDOORI CHICKEN
MARINATED IN YOGURT AND INDIAN SPICES

PREP TIME: 20 minutes
MARINATING TIME: 6 to 12 hours
GRILLING TIME: 35 to 58 minutes
SPECIAL EQUIPMENT: poultry shears

Marinade

- 1 cup plain yogurt
- ¼ cup fresh lemon juice
- 1 tablespoon minced fresh ginger
- 1 tablespoon minced garlic
- 1 tablespoon paprika
- 2 teaspoons ground cumin
- 2 teaspoons kosher salt
- 1 teaspoon ground turmeric
- ½ teaspoon ground cayenne pepper

- 1 whole chicken, 4 to 5 pounds
  Vegetable oil

1. In a large glass or stainless steel bowl, combine the marinade ingredients.

2. Cut the chicken into six pieces: two breast pieces, two whole leg (thigh and drumstick) pieces, and two wings. Remove and discard the skin from the breast and whole leg pieces. Using poultry shears, remove and discard the wing tips. Cut three or four slashes, about ½ inch deep, into the meatier side of the breast and whole leg pieces. Add the chicken to the marinade and turn to coat evenly. Cover and refrigerate for 6 to 12 hours.

3. Prepare the grill for direct and indirect cooking over medium heat (350° to 450°F).

4. Remove the chicken from the bowl and wipe off most of the marinade. Discard any remaining marinade. Lightly brush the chicken with oil.

5. Brush the cooking grates clean. Grill the chicken, with the meatier sides facing down first, over **direct medium heat**, with the lid closed, until grill marks form and the chicken begins to brown, 5 to 8 minutes. Turn and move the chicken over **indirect medium heat**, close the lid, and cook until the juices run clear and the meat is opaque all the way to the bone. The breasts and wings will take 30 to 35 minutes and the whole legs will take 40 to 50 minutes. Remove from the grill and let rest for 3 to 5 minutes. Transfer to a platter and serve warm.

SERVES: 4

GARLIC CHICKEN
WITH ROSEMARY AND LEMON

PREP TIME: 20 minutes
MARINATING TIME: 30 minutes to 2 hours
GRILLING TIME: 48 minutes to 1 hour

Paste

- 2 tablespoons extra-virgin olive oil
- 4 teaspoons finely chopped fresh rosemary leaves
- 1 teaspoon finely grated lemon zest
- 1 tablespoon fresh lemon juice
- 1 tablespoon minced garlic
- 1 teaspoon kosher salt
- ¼ teaspoon ground black pepper

- 4 whole chicken legs, 10 to 12 ounces each, trimmed of excess fat and skin

1. In a small bowl combine the paste ingredients. Using your fingertips, gently loosen the skin of the chicken legs and rub some of the paste under the skin of each leg. Rub the remaining paste all over both sides of the chicken. Cover and marinate at room temperature for 30 minutes or in the refrigerator for up to 2 hours.

2. Prepare the grill for direct and indirect cooking over medium heat (350°F to 450°F).

3. Brush the cooking grates clean. Grill the chicken, skin side down first, over *direct medium heat*, with the lid closed as much as possible, until golden brown, 8 to 10 minutes, turning occasionally. Then move the chicken over *indirect medium heat*, close the lid, and continue to grill until the juices run clear and the meat is no longer pink at the bone, 40 to 50 minutes. Remove from the grill and let rest for 3 to 5 minutes. Serve warm. Serving suggestion: Grecian Orzo Salad (for recipe, see page 125).

SERVES: 4

BARBECUED CHICKEN
WITH BOURBON-BACON SAUCE

PREP TIME: 10 minutes, plus about 20 minutes
for the sauce
MARINATING TIME: 8 to 24 hours
GRILLING TIME: 50 minutes to 1 hour

Sauce

- 4 slices bacon, cut into ½-inch dice
- 1 cup finely chopped yellow onion
- 1 tablespoon minced garlic
- ½ cup ketchup
- ¼ cup dark molasses
- ¼ cup yellow mustard
- ¼ cup bourbon
- 2 tablespoons brown sugar
- 2 tablespoons Worcestershire sauce
- ⅛ teaspoon Tabasco® sauce

- 4 whole chicken legs, 10 to 12 ounces each,
  trimmed of excess fat and skin

- 2 handfuls hickory wood chips, soaked in water
  for at least 30 minutes

1. In a medium saucepan over medium heat, cook the bacon until crisp, about 10 minutes, stirring occasionally. Reduce the heat to low, add the onion and garlic, and cook until soft, about 5 minutes. Add the remaining sauce ingredients and simmer for about 5 minutes. You should have about 2 cups of sauce. Remove from the heat and let cool.

2. Place the chicken in a large, resealable plastic bag and pour in 1 cup of the cooled sauce. Press the air out of the bag and seal tightly. Turn the bag to distribute the sauce. Refrigerate for at least 8 hours or up to 24 hours.

3. Remove the chicken from the bag and let the sauce cling to the chicken. Discard the sauce in the bag.

4. Prepare the grill for indirect cooking over medium heat (350° to 450°F).

5. Brush the cooking grates clean. Drain and scatter the wood chips over lit charcoal or put them in the smoker box of a gas grill, following manufacturer's instructions. Grill the chicken legs, skin side down, over *indirect medium heat*, with the lid closed, for 25 to 30 minutes. Then brush both sides with a thin layer of the sauce and continue cooking until the juices run clear and the meat is no longer pink at the bone, 25 to 30 minutes, occasionally turning and brushing with the sauce. Remove from the grill and let rest for 3 to 5 minutes. Serve warm with the remaining sauce on the side.

SERVES: 4

GRILLED CHICKEN ADOBO
WITH VINEGAR AND SOY SAUCE

PREP TIME: 20 minutes, plus time to cook the rice
GRILLING TIME: about 45 minutes
SPECIAL EQUIPMENT: 10-inch Dutch oven or large ovenproof saucepan

Sauce

- 2 tablespoons canola oil
- 1 small yellow onion, finely chopped
- 3 garlic cloves, thinly sliced
- ¾ cup cider vinegar
- ¾ cup water
- ½ cup low-sodium soy sauce
- 1 teaspoon ground black pepper
- 1 bay leaf

- 4 whole chicken legs, 10 to 12 ounces each, cut into thighs and drumsticks, trimmed of excess fat and skin
- ¼ cup canola oil
- 4 cups cooked white rice

1. Prepare the grill for direct cooking over medium heat (350° to 450°F) and low heat (250° to 350°F).

2. In a 10-inch Dutch oven or large ovenproof saucepan over *direct medium heat*, heat the oil. Add the onion and garlic and cook until golden brown, about 5 minutes, stirring occasionally to prevent burning. Add the remaining sauce ingredients. Place the thighs and drumsticks in a single layer on top of the sauce. Close the lid and cook until the liquid reaches a simmer. Then slide the pan over *direct low heat* to maintain the simmer. Simmer the chicken in the sauce for 30 minutes, with the lid closed as much as possible, turning the chicken pieces once.

3. Remove the chicken and bay leaf from the pan. Discard the bay leaf and lightly coat the chicken all over with oil.

4. At this point you should have about 1 cup of sauce remaining in the pan. If you have more than that, leave the pan over *direct low heat* and let the sauce reduce to about 1 cup. Then remove the pan from the grill.

5. Grill the chicken over *direct medium heat*, with the lid closed as much as possible, until lightly charred on all sides, 6 to 8 minutes, turning once or twice.

6. Return the chicken pieces to the pan and turn to coat them in the sauce. Serve the chicken warm with the rice and some sauce spooned over the top.

SERVES: 4

SKILLET-ROASTED CHICKEN
WITH FRESH THYME AND GARLIC POTATOES

PREP TIME: 20 minutes
GRILLING TIME: 50 minutes to 1 hour
SPECIAL EQUIPMENT: 10-inch cast-iron skillet

Paste

- 3 tablespoons extra-virgin olive oil
- 2 tablespoons finely chopped fresh thyme leaves
- 1 tablespoon finely chopped garlic
- 1 tablespoon Dijon mustard
- 1½ teaspoons kosher salt
- ½ teaspoon ground black pepper

- 12 red new potatoes, each 1½ to 2 inches in diameter, about 1¼ pounds total
- 4 chicken thighs (with bone and skin), 5 to 6 ounces each, trimmed of excess fat and skin
- 4 chicken drumsticks, 4 to 6 ounces each, trimmed of excess fat and skin

1. Prepare the grill for indirect cooking over medium heat (350° to 450°F).

2. In a small bowl mix the paste ingredients.

3. Quarter each potato and then place the potatoes in a large bowl. Add about half of the paste to the bowl and mix to coat the potatoes evenly. Spread the potatoes in a single layer in a 10-inch cast-iron skillet.

4. Add the thighs and drumsticks to the large bowl and add the remaining paste. Smear the paste evenly all over the chicken. Arrange the chicken pieces, skin side up, on top of the potatoes. It is okay for the pieces to touch, but don't cram them together.

5. Place the skillet over **indirect medium heat**, close the lid, and cook for 30 minutes. Then turn over each piece of chicken. Continue to cook until the chicken is golden brown on the surface and opaque all the way to the bone, 20 to 30 minutes.

6. Remove the chicken from the skillet and check to see if the potatoes are done. They should be brown around the edges and tender all the way to the center. If not, move the skillet over **direct medium heat** and continue to cook them for about 5 minutes, stirring gently so they don't collapse. When the potatoes are ready, lift them from the skillet with a slotted spoon and serve warm with the chicken.

SERVES: 4

GINGER-MARINATED DRUMSTICKS
WITH COCONUT MILK AND HONEY

PREP TIME: 10 minutes
MARINATING TIME: 6 to 24 hours
GRILLING TIME: 40 to 50 minutes

Marinade

- 1 cup loosely packed fresh cilantro leaves and tender stems
- 10 garlic cloves
- 1 four-inch section fresh ginger, cut into thin slices
- 1 can (13.5 ounces) unsweetened coconut milk, stirred
- ¾ cup low-sodium soy sauce
- ¼ cup honey

- 12 chicken drumsticks, about 4 ounces each, trimmed of excess fat and skin

NOTE!
You can also marinate the drumsticks in two large, resealable plastic bags.

1. In the bowl of a food processor fitted with a metal blade, combine the cilantro, garlic, and ginger. Process until the ingredients are finely chopped. Transfer to a large bowl and add the remaining marinade ingredients. Mix well. Add the drumsticks and rub the marinade into all sides with your hands. Cover the bowl and refrigerate for 6 to 24 hours.

2. Prepare the grill for indirect cooking over medium heat (350° to 450°F).

3. Remove the drumsticks from the bowl and discard the marinade. Brush the cooking grates clean. Grill the drumsticks over *indirect medium heat*, with the lid closed as much as possible, until the juices run clear and the meat is no longer pink at the bone, 40 to 50 minutes, turning once or twice. Remove from the grill and let rest for 3 to 5 minutes. Serve warm or at room temperature.

SERVES: 4 to 6

ANCHO CHILE CHICKEN THIGHS
WITH TOMATO CHUTNEY

PREP TIME: 20 minutes, plus 25 to 35 minutes for the chutney
GRILLING TIME: 36 to 40 minutes

Chutney

- 1 can (14 ounces) peeled diced tomatoes with juice
- ½ cup minced red onion
- ⅓ cup cider vinegar
- ⅓ cup light brown sugar
- 1 tablespoon balsamic vinegar
- 1 teaspoon kosher salt
- ¼ teaspoon crushed red pepper flakes

- ¼ cup dried currants or raisins

Rub

- 2 teaspoons ancho chile powder
- 1 teaspoon paprika
- 1 teaspoon kosher salt
- ½ teaspoon ground black pepper

- 8 chicken thighs (with bone and skin), 5 to 6 ounces each, trimmed of excess fat and skin

1. In a small saucepan over high heat, combine the chutney ingredients and cook until the mixture begins to boil. Reduce the heat to low, and simmer until almost all of the liquid has evaporated and it is thick and syrupy, 20 to 30 minutes. Remove the saucepan from the heat, mix in the currants, and let the chutney cool to room temperature before serving.

2. Prepare the grill for direct and indirect cooking over medium heat (350° to 450°F).

3. In a small bowl mix the rub ingredients. Season the thighs evenly with the rub.

4. Brush the cooking grates clean. Grill the thighs, skin side down first, over **direct medium heat**, until golden brown, 6 to 10 minutes, turning occasionally. Then move the thighs over **indirect medium heat** and cook until the juices run clear and the meat is no longer pink at the bone, about 30 minutes. Keep the lid closed as much as possible during grilling. Remove from the grill and let rest for 3 to 5 minutes. Serve warm with the chutney.

SERVES: 4 to 6

What are currants? Really they are just a small version of raisins made from Zante grapes.

SPICY CHICKEN THIGHS
WITH CITRUS-FENNEL RELISH

PREP TIME: 45 minutes
MARINATING TIME: 1 to 2 hours
GRILLING TIME: 36 to 40 minutes

Marinade

Finely grated zest and juice of 1 orange
3 tablespoons extra-virgin olive oil
1 tablespoon dried oregano
2 teaspoons kosher salt
1 teaspoon ground cayenne pepper

8 chicken thighs (with bone and skin), 5 to 6
ounces each, trimmed of excess fat and skin

Relish

1 lime
3 oranges, about 8 ounces each
½ small fennel bulb, cored and very thinly sliced,
about ½ cup
2 tablespoons finely chopped fresh Italian
parsley leaves
½ teaspoon reserved finely grated lime zest
1 teaspoon honey
⅛ teaspoon kosher salt

1. In a medium glass or stainless steel bowl, whisk the marinade ingredients. Add the thighs and turn to coat them evenly. Cover and refrigerate for 1 to 2 hours.

2. Finely grate enough zest from the lime to make ½ teaspoon and set aside. With a sharp knife, cut a thin slice from the top and bottom of each orange. Set the orange on one end and carefully slice from top to bottom following the curve of the orange to remove the peel and pith. Remove the segments by carefully sliding the knife down one side of each orange segment and then the other. Cut the segments into ½-inch chunks. Repeat with the lime. Put the orange and lime segments in a medium glass or stainless steel bowl, and add the rest of the relish ingredients. Gently stir to combine. Let stand at room temperature until ready to serve.

3. Prepare the grill for direct and indirect cooking over medium heat (350° to 450°F).

4. Brush the cooking grates clean. Remove the thighs from the bowl, letting the excess marinade drip back into the bowl. Discard the marinade. Grill the thighs, skin side down first, over *direct medium heat*, with the lid closed as much as possible, until golden brown, 6 to 10 minutes, turning occasionally. Move the thighs over *indirect medium heat* and continue to grill, with the lid closed, until the juices run clear and the meat is no longer pink at the bone, about 30 minutes. Remove from the grill and let rest for 3 to 5 minutes. Serve warm with the relish.

SERVES: 4 to 6

40

MOROCCAN CHICKEN THIGHS
MARINATED IN RED PEPPER PASTE

PREP TIME: 30 minutes
MARINATING TIME: 8 to 24 hours
GRILLING TIME: 36 to 40 minutes

Paste

3 garlic cloves
3 medium roasted red bell peppers (from a jar), drained
2 tablespoons extra-virgin olive oil
2 teaspoons coriander seed
2 teaspoons caraway seed
1 teaspoon cumin seed
1 teaspoon ground black pepper
¾ teaspoon kosher salt
¼ teaspoon ground cayenne pepper

8 chicken thighs (with bone and skin), 5 to 6 ounces each, trimmed of excess fat and skin

1. In a blender or food processor, mince the garlic, and then add the remaining paste ingredients. If the paste is too thick, add about 1 tablespoon of water.

2. Put the thighs in a large, resealable plastic bag and add the paste. Press the air out of the bag and seal tightly. Turn the bag to distribute the paste and refrigerate for 8 to 24 hours.

3. Prepare the grill for direct and indirect cooking over medium heat (350° to 450°F).

4. Remove the thighs from the bag and discard the paste. Brush the cooking grates clean. Grill the thighs, skin side down first, over **direct medium heat**, until golden brown, 6 to 10 minutes, turning occasionally. Move the thighs over **indirect medium heat** and continue to cook until the juices run clear and the meat is no longer pink at the bone, about 30 minutes. Keep the lid closed as much as possible during grilling. Remove from the grill and let rest for 3 to 5 minutes. Serve warm.

SERVES: 4 to 6

THIGHS AND DRUMSTICKS
WITH ROOT BEER BARBECUE SAUCE

PREP TIME: 20 minutes, plus about 35 minutes for the sauce
MARINATING TIME: up to 2 hours
GRILLING TIME: 36 to 40 minutes

Sauce

- 1 tablespoon extra-virgin olive oil
- 1 cup finely chopped yellow onion
- 1 teaspoon minced garlic
- ½ teaspoon grated fresh ginger
- 1 cup root beer
- 1 cup ketchup
- ½ cup fresh orange juice
- 2 tablespoons Worcestershire sauce
- 2 tablespoons light brown sugar

- ½ teaspoon grated lemon zest
- Kosher salt
- Ground black pepper

Rub

- 1½ teaspoons paprika
- 1 teaspoon prepared chili powder
- 1 teaspoon kosher salt
- ½ teaspoon ground black pepper

- 4 chicken thighs (with bone and skin), 5 to 6 ounces each, trimmed of excess fat and skin
- 4 chicken drumsticks, 3 to 4 ounces each, trimmed of excess fat and skin
- Extra-virgin olive oil

1. In a medium saucepan over medium heat, warm the oil. Add the onion and cook until tender but not browned, 3 to 4 minutes, stirring occasionally. Add the garlic and ginger and cook until fragrant, about 1 minute. Add the remaining sauce ingredients. Whisk until smooth, and simmer over medium-low heat until the sauce is thick and coats the back of a wooden spoon, 20 to 30 minutes, stirring occasionally. Remove the saucepan from the heat and stir in the lemon zest. Season with salt and pepper. Divide the sauce and use about 1 cup for basting the chicken and the rest for serving.

2. In a small bowl mix the rub ingredients. Lightly brush the chicken pieces all over with oil and season evenly with the rub. Refrigerate until ready to grill (but no more than 2 hours).

3. Prepare the grill for direct and indirect cooking over medium heat (350° to 450°F).

4. Brush the cooking grates clean. Grill the chicken, skin side down first, over ***direct medium heat***, with the lid closed as much as possible, until golden brown, 6 to 10 minutes, turning occasionally. Move the chicken over ***indirect medium heat***, close the lid, and cook for about 10 minutes. Then brush both sides with a thin layer of the sauce. Continue cooking over ***indirect medium heat***, with the lid closed as much as possible, until the juices run clear and the meat is no longer pink at the bone, about 20 minutes more, occasionally turning and brushing with the sauce. Remove from the grill and let rest for 3 to 5 minutes. Serve warm with the reserved sauce.

SERVES: 4

42

OAK-SMOKED THIGHS
WITH HOISIN GLAZE

PREP TIME: 10 minutes
GRILLING TIME: 36 to 40 minutes

Glaze

- ¼ cup hoisin sauce
- ¼ cup ketchup
- 1 tablespoon cider vinegar

- 8 skinless chicken thighs (with bone),
  5 to 6 ounces each, trimmed of excess fat
- 2 teaspoons kosher salt
- ½ teaspoon ground black pepper

- 2 handfuls oak wood chips, soaked in water for
  at least 30 minutes

1. In a small glass or stainless steel bowl, whisk the glaze ingredients.

2. Season the thighs evenly with the salt and pepper.

3. Prepare the grill for direct and indirect cooking over medium heat (350° to 450°F).

4. Brush the cooking grates clean. Grill the thighs, smooth (skin) side down first, over ***direct medium heat***, with the lid closed as much as possible, until golden brown, 6 to 10 minutes, turning occasionally. Then move the thighs over ***indirect medium heat*** and lightly brush both sides with some of the glaze.

5. Drain and scatter the wood chips over the lit charcoal or put them in the smoker box of a gas grill, following manufacturer's instructions. Continue grilling the chicken over ***indirect medium heat***, with the lid closed as much as possible, until the juices run clear and the meat is no longer pink at the bone, about 30 minutes, occasionally turning and brushing with the glaze. Remove from the grill and let rest for 3 to 5 minutes. Serve warm.

SERVES: 4

CHICKEN BREASTS
WITH LIME CREMA

PREP TIME: 20 minutes
GRILLING TIME: 23 to 35 minutes

Crema
- ¼ cup sour cream
- 2 tablespoons finely chopped fresh cilantro leaves
- 4 teaspoons fresh lime juice
- ⅛ teaspoon kosher salt

Paste
- 2 tablespoons extra-virgin olive oil
- 4 teaspoons prepared chili powder
- ¾ teaspoon onion powder
- ¾ teaspoon chipotle chile powder
- ½ teaspoon kosher salt
- ¼ teaspoon ground black pepper

- 4 chicken breast halves (with bone and skin), 10 to 12 ounces each

1. In a small glass or stainless steel bowl, whisk the crema ingredients. Cover and refrigerate until ready to serve.

2. Prepare the grill for direct and indirect cooking over medium heat (350° to 450°F).

3. In a small bowl combine the paste ingredients. Using your fingertips, carefully lift the skin from the chicken breasts, leaving the skin closest to the breastbone attached. Rub 1 teaspoon of the paste under the skin all over the exposed meat. Lay the skin back in place and spread the remaining paste evenly over all the chicken breasts.

4. Brush the cooking grates clean. Grill the chicken, skin side down, over ***direct medium heat***, with the lid closed, until the skin is browned, 3 to 5 minutes. Turn over the chicken and move over ***indirect medium heat***. Close the lid and continue to cook until the meat is opaque all the way to the bone, 20 to 30 minutes. Remove from the grill and let rest for 3 to 5 minutes. Serve warm with the crema. Serving suggestion: Corn and Black Bean Salad (for recipe, see page 123).

SERVES: 4

CHICKEN BREASTS
WITH SMOKED PAPRIKA BUTTER

PREP TIME: 15 minutes
GRILLING TIME: 23 to 35 minutes
SPECIAL EQUIPMENT: spice mill

Butter
- 2 teaspoons coriander seed or 1 tablespoon ground coriander
- ½ cup (1 stick) unsalted butter, softened
- 2 teaspoons smoked paprika
- ¼ teaspoon ground cayenne pepper

- 6 chicken breast halves (with bone and skin), 10 to 12 ounces each
- 2 teaspoons kosher salt
- 1 teaspoon ground black pepper

Smoked paprika is made from brilliantly red pimento peppers dried slowly over oak wood and ground for easy use.

1. In a small skillet over medium heat, toast the coriander seed until aromatic and slightly darker in color, about 2 minutes, stirring occasionally. Pulse in a spice mill until ground.

2. In a small bowl mix the butter ingredients. Divide the butter and reserve half.

3. Prepare the grill for direct and indirect cooking over medium heat (350° to 450°F).

4. Using your fingertips, carefully lift the skin from the chicken breasts, leaving the skin closest to the breastbone attached. Rub the butter evenly under the skin all over the exposed meat. Lay the skin back in place. Season evenly with the salt and pepper.

5. Brush the cooking grates clean. Grill the chicken, skin side down, over ***direct medium heat***, with the lid closed, until the skin is browned, 3 to 5 minutes. Turn over the chicken and move over ***indirect medium heat***. Close the lid and continue to cook until the meat is opaque all the way to the bone, 20 to 30 minutes. Remove from the grill and let rest for 3 to 5 minutes. Smear the reserved butter over the chicken. Serve warm. Serving suggestion: Grill-Roasted New Potatoes (for recipe, see page 120).

SERVES: 6

46

CAJUN CHICKEN BREASTS
WITH GRILLED CORN AND BLACK-EYED PEA SALSA

PREP TIME: 15 minutes
GRILLING TIME: 33 to 50 minutes

Rub

- 1 teaspoon granulated garlic
- 1 teaspoon granulated onion
- 1 teaspoon dried thyme
- 1 teaspoon dried oregano
- 1 teaspoon kosher salt
- 1 teaspoon paprika
- ¾ teaspoon light brown sugar
- ½ teaspoon smoked paprika
- ½ teaspoon ground black pepper

- 4 chicken breast halves (with bone and skin),
  10 to 12 ounces each
  Extra-virgin olive oil

Salsa

- 2 ears fresh corn, husked
- 1 can (15 ounces) black-eyed peas or white navy
  beans, rinsed
- ½ cup slivered red onion
- ½ cup finely chopped red bell pepper
- 2 tablespoons extra-virgin olive oil
- 1 tablespoon white wine vinegar
- ½ teaspoon Tabasco® sauce
  Kosher salt
  Ground black pepper

1. Prepare the grill for direct and indirect cooking over medium heat (350° to 450°F).

2. In a small bowl mix the rub ingredients.

3. Lightly brush the chicken breasts on both sides with oil and season them evenly with the rub. Lightly coat the corn with oil.

4. Brush the cooking grates clean. Grill the corn over *direct medium heat*, with the lid closed as much as possible, until browned in spots and tender, 10 to 15 minutes, turning occasionally. Remove from the grill and, when cool enough to handle, cut the kernels off the cobs. Put the kernels in a medium bowl and add the black-eyed peas, onion, and bell pepper.

5. Grill the chicken, skin side down, over *direct medium heat*, with the lid closed, until the skin is golden brown, 3 to 5 minutes. Turn over the chicken and continue to cook over *indirect medium heat*, with the lid closed, until the meat is opaque all the way to the bone, 20 to 30 minutes. Remove from the grill and let rest while you finish the salsa.

6. In a small glass or stainless steel bowl, whisk the oil, vinegar, and Tabasco sauce. Add to the corn mixture. Stir gently to combine. Season with salt and pepper. Serve the chicken warm with the salsa.

SERVES: 4

CHINESE CHICKEN WINGS
WITH HONEY AND SOY GLAZE

PREP TIME: 20 minutes
GRILLING TIME: 20 to 35 minutes

Glaze
⅓ cup low-sodium soy sauce
⅓ cup water
¼ cup honey
2 tablespoons rice vinegar
1 teaspoon grated fresh ginger
¼ teaspoon Chinese five-spice powder
¼ teaspoon ground cayenne pepper
½ teaspoon toasted sesame oil

Rub
1 teaspoon granulated garlic
½ teaspoon kosher salt
½ teaspoon ground black pepper

12 chicken wings, about 2 pounds total,
   wing tips removed

1. Prepare the grill for direct and indirect cooking over medium heat (350° to 450°F).

2. In a small saucepan over medium-high heat, combine the soy sauce, water, honey, vinegar, ginger, five-spice powder, and cayenne pepper; bring to a boil. Reduce the heat and simmer until you have ½ cup of liquid, 5 to 10 minutes. Remove from the heat and add the sesame oil.

3. In a small bowl mix the rub ingredients. Season the wings evenly with the rub.

4. Brush the cooking grates clean. Grill the wings over *direct medium heat*, with the lid closed as much as possible, until golden brown all over, 10 to 15 minutes, turning once or twice. Then move the wings over *indirect medium heat* and lightly brush them with some of the glaze. Close the lid and continue grilling until the skin is dark brown and the meat is no longer pink at the bone, 10 to 20 minutes, turning and basting with the glaze once or twice. If desired, during the final few minutes, move the wings over *direct medium heat* to crisp the skin a bit more, turning once or twice. Remove from the grill and serve warm.

SERVES: 4 (as an appetizer)

HOT WINGS
WITH BLUE CHEESE DRESSING

PREP TIME: 20 minutes
MARINATING TIME: 1 hour
GRILLING TIME: 22 to 24 minutes

Paste

- 4 teaspoons minced canned chipotle chiles in adobo
- 2 teaspoons kosher salt
- 1½ teaspoons paprika
- 1 teaspoon garlic powder
- 1 teaspoon onion powder
- 1 teaspoon ground black pepper

- 16 chicken wings, about 2½ pounds total, each one cut in half at the joint, wing tips removed

Hot sauce

- 3 tablespoons extra-virgin olive oil
- 1 garlic clove, grated or minced
- 4 teaspoons cider vinegar
- 2½ teaspoons Tabasco® sauce
  Kosher salt
  Ground black pepper

Dressing

- ¼ cup crumbled blue cheese
- 2 tablespoons sour cream
- 2 tablespoons mayonnaise
- 1 tablespoon buttermilk
- ½ teaspoon cider vinegar

1. In a large bowl combine the paste ingredients. Add the wings and stir to coat them all over with the paste. Cover and refrigerate for 1 hour.

2. In a heavy, small saucepan over medium heat, warm the oil. Add the garlic and stir until aromatic, about 1 minute. Add the vinegar and Tabasco sauce and simmer for 1 minute. Season with salt and pepper. Transfer to large glass or stainless steel bowl.

3. In a medium bowl combine the dressing ingredients. Cover and chill until ready to serve.

4. Prepare the grill for direct and indirect cooking over medium-high heat (about 450°F).

5. Brush the cooking grates clean. Remove the wings from the bowl and wipe off most of the paste. Grill the wings over ***direct medium-high heat*** until grill marks appear, about 4 minutes, turning once. Move the wings over ***indirect medium-high heat*** and continue grilling until the meat is no longer pink at the bone and the skin is crisp, about 15 minutes, turning occasionally. Keep the lid closed as much as possible during grilling. Transfer the wings to the bowl with the hot sauce; turn to coat. Return the wings to the grill and cook over ***direct medium-high heat*** for an additional 3 to 5 minutes, turning once or twice. Remove from the grill and serve with the blue cheese dressing.

SERVES: 6 to 8 (as an appetizer)

BLUE CHEESE CHICKEN PATTY MELTS
WITH GRILLED ONIONS

PREP TIME: 15 minutes
GRILLING TIME: 19 to 24 minutes

1½ pounds ground chicken (preferably thigh meat)
¼ cup mayonnaise
4 teaspoons Dijon mustard
1 large sweet yellow onion, cut crosswise into
   ¼-inch slices
   Extra-virgin olive oil
   Kosher salt
   Ground black pepper
4 slices blue cheese, each about 1 ounce
8 slices rye bread

1. Shape the ground chicken into four equal-sized patties, each about ¾ inch thick. With your thumb or the back of a spoon, make a shallow indentation about 1 inch wide in the center of each patty so the centers are about ½ inch thick. This will help the patties cook evenly and prevent them from puffing on the grill. Cover the patties with plastic wrap and refrigerate until you are ready to grill them, or for at least 5 minutes.

2. In a small bowl mix the mayonnaise and mustard.

3. Prepare the grill for direct cooking over medium heat (350° to 450°F).

4. Lightly coat the onion slices on both sides with oil and season with salt and pepper. Brush the cooking grates clean. Grill over *direct medium heat*, with the lid closed as much as possible, until tender, 6 to 8 minutes, turning once. Remove from the grill.

5. Lightly brush the patties on both sides with oil and season evenly with salt and pepper. Grill over *direct medium heat*, with the lid closed as much as possible, until fully cooked but still juicy, 12 to 14 minutes, turning once. During the last 2 to 3 minutes of grilling time, place a slice of cheese on top of each patty. Transfer the patties to a platter.

6. Brush the bread on one side with some oil and toast the slices over *direct medium heat* until browned on both sides, 1 to 2 minutes, turning once. Serve the burgers on rye with the mayonnaise mixture and some onions on top.

SERVES: 4

52

SOUTHWESTERN GREEN CHILE CHICKEN CHEESEBURGERS

PREP TIME: 15 minutes
GRILLING TIME: 12 to 14 minutes

Burgers

- 1 pound ground chicken (preferably thigh meat)
- 1 cup plain bread crumbs
- 1 can (4 ounces) diced, fire-roasted mild green chiles
- ¼ cup minced yellow onion
- 1 large egg
- 1 teaspoon dried mustard
- 1 teaspoon ancho chile powder
- 1 teaspoon granulated garlic
- ½ teaspoon kosher salt
- ½ teaspoon paprika
- ¼ teaspoon ground cumin
- ¼ teaspoon ground black pepper

- Extra-virgin olive oil
- 4 whole-grain hamburger buns
- 4 thin slices sharp cheddar cheese
- 4 lettuce leaves
- Ketchup (optional)

1. Prepare the grill for direct cooking over medium heat (350° to 450°F).

2. In a large bowl gently combine the burger ingredients and form into four patties of equal size and thickness, each about ¾ inch thick (the patties will be soft). With your thumb or the back of a spoon, make a shallow indentation about 1 inch wide in the center of each patty so the centers are about ½ inch thick. This will help the patties cook evenly and prevent them from puffing on the grill. Brush both sides of each patty with oil.

3. Brush the cooking grates clean. Grill the patties over *direct medium heat*, with the lid closed as much as possible, until fully cooked but still juicy, 12 to 14 minutes, turning once. During the last minute of grilling time, toast the buns, cut sides down, over *direct medium heat* and top each patty with a slice of cheese. Remove the patties and buns from the grill and top the burgers with the lettuce and ketchup, if desired. Serve warm.

SERVES: 4

CHICKEN BURGERS
WITH GRILLED MUSHROOMS AND ROSEMARY AIOLI

PREP TIME: 20 minutes
GRILLING TIME: 20 to 26 minutes

Aioli
- ½ cup mayonnaise
- 1 teaspoon minced garlic
- 1 teaspoon minced fresh rosemary leaves
- 1 tablespoon extra-virgin olive oil
- Kosher salt
- Ground black pepper

- 1½ pounds ground chicken (preferably thigh meat)
- 2 large portabello mushrooms, cleaned, stems and black gills removed
- Extra-virgin olive oil
- 4 thin slices sharp cheddar cheese
- 4 hamburger buns
- 4 butter lettuce leaves
- 1 large tomato, cut into 4 slices

1. Prepare the grill for direct cooking over medium heat (350° to 450°F).

2. In a small bowl whisk the mayonnaise, garlic, rosemary, and oil. Season with salt and pepper.

3. In a medium bowl gently combine the chicken with 2 tablespoons of the aioli. Shape into four patties of equal size and thickness, each about ¾ inch thick. With your thumb or the back of a spoon, make a shallow indentation about 1 inch wide in the center of each patty so the centers are about ½ inch thick. This will help the patties cook evenly on the grill.

4. Lightly brush the mushrooms with oil and season with salt and pepper. Brush the cooking grates clean. Grill the mushrooms, gill sides down, over ***direct medium heat***, with the lid closed as much as possible, until they begin to soften, 4 to 6 minutes. Brush the mushrooms with more oil, turn them over, and cook until they are tender when pierced with the tip of a knife, 4 to 6 minutes. Transfer the mushrooms to a work surface and cut into ⅓-inch-thick slices.

5. Grill the patties over ***direct medium heat***, with the lid closed as much as possible, until fully cooked but still juicy, 12 to 14 minutes, turning once. During the last minute of grilling time, toast the buns, cut sides down, over ***direct medium heat*** and top each patty with sliced mushrooms and cheese.

6. Remove the patties and buns from the grill and top the burgers with the lettuce and tomato and the remaining aioli. Serve warm.

SERVES: 4

CHICKEN THIGHS
SMOTHERED IN CORN AND BACON RELISH

PREP TIME: 10 minutes, plus about 25 minutes for the relish
GRILLING TIME: 18 to 25 minutes

  6 slices bacon, cut crosswise into ⅓-inch pieces
  1 medium Anaheim chile pepper, finely chopped
  ½ cup finely chopped yellow onion
  ½ teaspoon dried thyme
  ⅛ teaspoon ground black pepper
  ½ teaspoon sherry vinegar
  2 ears fresh corn, husked
      Extra-virgin olive oil

  8 boneless, skinless chicken thighs, about 4 ounces each
  ¾ teaspoon kosher salt
  ¾ teaspoon dried thyme
  ½ teaspoon ground black pepper

1. In a large skillet over medium heat, arrange the bacon in a single layer and cook until brown and crispy, 10 to 15 minutes, stirring occasionally. With a slotted spoon, lift the bacon pieces from the skillet and put them in a bowl, leaving the bacon fat in the skillet. Add the chopped chile pepper, onion, thyme, and pepper to the skillet. Cook over medium heat until the onions are browned and tender, 8 to 10 minutes, stirring occasionally to prevent burning. Add the vinegar. Return the bacon to the skillet. Mix well and set aside.

2. Prepare the grill for direct cooking over medium heat (350° to 450°F).

3. Brush the cooking grates clean. Lightly brush the corn with oil. Grill the corn over ***direct medium heat***, with the lid closed as much as possible, until browned in spots and tender, 10 to 15 minutes, turning occasionally. Remove from the grill and let cool. Cut the kernels off the cobs and mix them with the bacon mixture.

4. Lightly brush the thighs on both sides with oil and season evenly with the salt, thyme, and pepper. Grill the thighs over ***direct medium heat***, with the lid closed as much as possible, until the meat is firm and the juices run clear, 8 to 10 minutes, turning once or twice. Reheat the relish in the skillet over medium heat. Transfer the chicken to a cutting board and cut into ¾-inch strips. Place the chicken strips on a platter and spoon the relish over the top. Serve warm.

SERVES: 4 to 6

LEMON CHICKEN AND MINT RISOTTO
WITH GREEN PEAS

PREP TIME: 1 hour
GRILLING TIME: 8 to 10 minutes
SPECIAL EQUIPMENT: 6-quart saucepan

Marinade

- 3 tablespoons extra-virgin olive oil
- 1 teaspoon finely grated lemon zest
- 2 tablespoons fresh lemon juice
- 1 tablespoon finely chopped fresh mint leaves
- 1 teaspoon minced garlic
- 1 teaspoon kosher salt
- ½ teaspoon ground black pepper

- 6 boneless, skinless chicken thighs, about 4 ounces each

Risotto

- 1 bag (1 pound) frozen peas, about 2½ cups
- 4½ cups low-sodium chicken broth
- 2 tablespoons extra-virgin olive oil
- ¼ cup minced shallots
- 1½ cups Arborio rice
- ½ cup finely chopped fresh mint leaves
- ½ cup mascarpone cheese
  Kosher salt
  Ground black pepper
- 1–2 tablespoons fresh lemon juice
- 1 lemon, quartered

1. In a small bowl whisk the marinade ingredients.

2. Place the thighs in a large, resealable plastic bag and pour in the marinade. Squeeze the air out of the bag and seal tightly. Refrigerate until ready to grill.

3. Thaw the peas under cool running water. Set aside. In a medium saucepan over medium heat, heat the broth until it simmers. Keep warm and covered.

4. Prepare the grill for direct cooking over medium heat (350° to 450°F).

5. In a 6-quart saucepan over medium heat, warm the oil. Add the shallots and cook until they are tender but not brown, 3 to 5 minutes. Add the rice and stir until coated with oil. With a ladle, add 1 cup of warm broth and cook, stirring frequently, until most of the liquid is absorbed. Add warm broth 1 cup at a time, cooking until the liquid is absorbed and the rice is tender but not mushy, 20 to 30 minutes. The mixture will be creamy. As the last round of broth is being absorbed, stir in the peas, mint, and cheese. Season with salt, pepper, and lemon juice. Remove from the heat and cover.

6. Brush the cooking grates clean. Remove the thighs from the bag and discard the marinade. Grill the thighs over ***direct medium heat***, with the lid closed as much as possible, until the meat is firm and the juices run clear, 8 to 10 minutes, turning once or twice. Transfer the thighs to a cutting board and cut into bite-sized pieces. Add them into the risotto and stir to combine. Serve the risotto warm with lemon wedges.

SERVES: 4

SMOKED CHICKEN CHILI
WITH CORN AND BEANS

PREP TIME: 15 minutes
GRILLING TIME: 30 to 35 minutes
SPECIAL EQUIPMENT: 12-inch cast-iron skillet

2 handfuls hickory wood chips, soaked in water
for at least 30 minutes

4 boneless, skinless chicken thighs,
about 4 ounces each
1 large red onion, cut crosswise into ½-inch slices
Extra-virgin olive oil
Kosher salt
Ground black pepper

2 teaspoons minced garlic
2 tablespoons flour
3 cups low-sodium chicken broth
2 cans (15 ounces each) kidney beans, rinsed
1½ cups corn kernels, fresh or frozen
1 tablespoon ancho chile powder
1 teaspoon dried oregano
½ teaspoon ground cumin

1. Prepare the grill for direct cooking over medium heat (350° to 450°F).

2. Drain and scatter the wood chips directly over lit charcoal or put them in the smoker box of a gas grill, following manufacturer's instructions.

3. Lightly coat the thighs and onion slices on both sides with oil and season with salt and pepper.

4. Brush the cooking grates clean. Grill the thighs and onions over *direct medium heat*, with the lid closed as much as possible, until the meat is firm and the juices run clear and the onions are tender, 8 to 10 minutes, turning once or twice. Transfer to a cutting board and cut the thighs and onions into ½-inch chunks.

5. In a 12-inch cast-iron skillet over *direct medium heat*, warm 2 tablespoons of oil. Add the garlic and cook until fragrant, about 1 minute, stirring frequently to prevent burning. Add the flour and immediately stir it into the oil. Cook for 1 to 2 minutes, stirring occasionally. Add the broth, beans, corn, chile powder, oregano, and cumin. Mix well and bring the liquid to a simmer (cover the skillet if necessary). Adjust the heat to keep the liquid at a simmer. Add the chicken and onions and cook until slightly thickened, 15 to 20 minutes. Season with salt and pepper. Remove from the heat and let cool for a few minutes. Serve warm.

SERVES: 4 to 6

INDIAN CHICKEN SKEWERS
WITH FRESH CILANTRO PUREE

PREP TIME: 35 minutes
MARINATING TIME: 2 to 4 hours
GRILLING TIME: 8 to 10 minutes
SPECIAL EQUIPMENT: metal or bamboo skewers (if using bamboo, soak in water for at least 30 minutes)

Paste

- ½ cup plain whole milk yogurt
- 2 teaspoons curry powder
- 2 teaspoons minced garlic
- 2 teaspoons minced fresh ginger
- 2 teaspoons kosher salt
- 1 teaspoon granulated sugar

- 10 boneless, skinless chicken thighs, about 4 ounces each, cut into 1½-inch pieces

Puree

- 2 cups loosely packed fresh cilantro leaves and tender stems
- 2 small serrano chile peppers, stemmed, seeded, and roughly chopped
- 3 tablespoons fresh lemon juice
- 1 tablespoon roughly chopped fresh ginger
- 1 tablespoon granulated sugar
- 1½ teaspoons kosher salt
- 2 garlic cloves, roughly chopped
  Extra-virgin olive oil

- 1 medium red onion

1. In a medium bowl whisk the paste ingredients. Place the chicken in a large, resealable plastic bag and add the paste. Press the air out of the bag and seal tightly. Knead the bag to distribute the paste and refrigerate for 2 to 4 hours.

2. In the bowl of a food processor or blender, process the puree ingredients except the oil. Then, with the motor running, slowly add 2 tablespoons of oil to make a smooth puree.

3. Prepare the grill for direct cooking over medium heat (350° to 450°F).

4. Cut the onion in half lengthwise and then cut each half into 6 wedges. Remove the chicken from the bag and discard the paste. Thread the chicken and onion leaves (use two or three outer leaves from each wedge) alternately onto skewers. Liberally brush the skewers all over with oil.

5. Brush the cooking grates clean. Grill the skewers over **direct medium heat**, with the lid closed as much as possible, until the meat is fully cooked but not dry, 8 to 10 minutes, turning once or twice. Serve warm with the cilantro puree on the side for dipping.

SERVES: 4 to 6

CHICKEN TACOS WITH GOAT CHEESE
AND ROASTED TOMATO-GARLIC SALSA

2 medium ripe tomatoes
½ medium white onion, quartered
1 medium red bell pepper
4 scallions, root ends trimmed
  Extra-virgin olive oil
2 garlic cloves
2 teaspoons minced canned chipotle chiles in adobo (or more, depending on how spicy you want your salsa)
1 teaspoon fresh lime juice
  Kosher salt

Rub

1 teaspoon kosher salt
1 teaspoon prepared chili powder
½ teaspoon ground black pepper

4 boneless, skinless chicken thighs, about 4 ounces each
  Fresh lime juice
8 small flour tortillas (6 inches)
½ cup crumbled fresh goat cheese

1. Prepare the grill for direct cooking over high heat (450° to 550°F).

2. Lightly brush the tomatoes, onion pieces, bell pepper, and scallions all over with oil. Brush the cooking grates clean. Grill the vegetables over *direct high heat*, with the lid closed as much as possible, until they are charred all over and tender, turning as needed. Remove the vegetables from the grill as they are done. The onion and bell pepper will take 10 to 12 minutes, the tomatoes will take 6 to 8 minutes, and the scallions will take 2 to 4 minutes. Place the bell pepper in a bowl and cover with plastic wrap. Let stand for 10 to 15 minutes.

3. In the bowl of a food processor or blender, process the tomatoes, onion, garlic, chipotle chiles, and lime juice until smooth. Season with salt. Pour the salsa into a glass or stainless steel bowl and set aside.

4. In a small bowl combine the rub ingredients. Lightly brush the thighs on both sides with oil and season evenly with the rub.

5. Brush the cooking grates clean. Grill the thighs over *direct high heat*, with the lid closed as much as possible, until the meat is firm and the juices run clear, 6 to 8 minutes, turning once or twice. Transfer to a cutting board and let cool.

6. When the thighs are cool enough to handle, cut them into ⅓-inch pieces and put them in a large bowl along with ⅓ cup of the salsa. Remove and discard the stem, skin, and seeds from the bell pepper. Chop the pepper and scallions and add them to the bowl; toss to combine. Season with salt and lime juice.

7. Heat the tortillas over ***direct high heat*** just to soften them, 30 seconds to 1 minute, turning once.

8. Lay the tortillas in a single layer on a work surface. Evenly divide the cheese and the chicken-vegetable mixture among the tortillas. Fold up the tortillas and serve with the remaining salsa on the side.

SERVES: 4

MOJITO CHICKEN BREASTS

PREP TIME: 10 minutes
MARINATING TIME: 1 to 2 hours
GRILLING TIME: 8 to 12 minutes

Marinade

- 1 teaspoon grated lime zest
- ¼ cup fresh lime juice
- ¼ cup extra-virgin olive oil
- 2 tablespoons light rum
- 2 tablespoons finely chopped fresh mint leaves
- 1 teaspoon kosher salt

- 4 boneless chicken breast halves (with skin), 6 to 8 ounces each
- 2 tablespoons finely chopped fresh mint leaves

1. In a medium bowl whisk the marinade ingredients.

2. Place the chicken in a large, resealable plastic bag and pour in the marinade. Press the air out of the bag and seal tightly. Turn the bag to distribute the marinade and refrigerate for 1 to 2 hours.

3. Prepare the grill for direct cooking over medium heat (350° to 450°F).

4. Remove the chicken from the bag, letting the excess marinade drip back into the bag. Discard the marinade.

5. Brush the cooking grates clean. Grill the chicken, skin side down first, over *direct medium heat*, with the lid closed as much as possible, until the meat is firm to the touch and opaque all the way to the center, 8 to 12 minutes, turning once or twice. Remove from the grill and let rest for 3 to 5 minutes. Serve warm garnished with a sprinkling of chopped mint. Serving suggestion: Roasted Corn and Black Bean Salad (for recipe, see page 123).

SERVES: 4

CHICKEN BREASTS
DRIZZLED WITH ORANGE-GINGER SAUCE

PREP TIME: 15 minutes
GRILLING TIME: 8 to 12 minutes

Rub
1 teaspoon dried thyme
1 teaspoon granulated garlic
1 teaspoon kosher salt
½ teaspoon ground black pepper

4 boneless chicken breast halves (with skin),
   6 to 8 ounces each
   Extra-virgin olive oil

Sauce
½ cup orange marmalade
2 tablespoons cider vinegar
1 tablespoon soy sauce
2 teaspoons grated fresh ginger
⅛ teaspoon ground black pepper

1. In a small bowl combine the rub ingredients.

2. Lightly brush the chicken on both sides with oil and season evenly with the rub. Cover with plastic wrap and allow to stand at room temperature for up to 30 minutes while you make the sauce.

3. Prepare the grill for direct cooking over medium heat (350° to 450°F).

4. In a small saucepan over medium heat, mix the sauce ingredients. Cook the sauce until liquefied and bubbling, 3 to 4 minutes, stirring occasionally. Remove from the heat and allow to cool to room temperature before serving.

5. Brush the cooking grates clean. Grill the chicken, skin side down first, over **direct medium heat**, with the lid closed as much as possible, until the meat is firm to the touch and opaque all the way to the center, 8 to 12 minutes, turning once or twice. Remove from the grill and let rest for 3 to 5 minutes. Cut the chicken into thin slices. Drizzle as much of the sauce as you like over the slices. Serve warm. Serving suggestion: Eggplant with Spicy Asian Dressing (for recipe, see page 114).

SERVES: 4

GRILLED CHICKEN PANZANELLA
WITH BASIL VINAIGRETTE

PREP TIME: 40 minutes
GRILLING TIME: 12 to 18 minutes

Dressing

- ½ cup loosely packed fresh basil leaves
- ¼ cup loosely packed fresh Italian parsley leaves and tender stems
- 1 tablespoon fresh lemon juice
- 1 tablespoon red wine vinegar
- 1 small garlic clove, minced
- ⅓ cup extra-virgin olive oil
- ½ teaspoon kosher salt
- ¼ teaspoon ground black pepper

- 3 medium summer squashes (such as zucchini and crookneck), cut lengthwise into ½-inch-thick slices
- 1 red bell pepper, cut lengthwise into ½-inch-thick slices
- ½ pound (½ loaf) country white bread, cut crosswise into 1-inch slices
  Extra-virgin olive oil
  Kosher salt
  Ground black pepper

- 2 boneless, skinless chicken breast halves, about 6 ounces each
- 1 pound tomatoes, cored, cut into ½-inch cubes
- ½ cup crumbled feta cheese

1. In the bowl of a food processor, pulse the basil, parsley, lemon juice, vinegar, and garlic until coarsely chopped. With the machine running, slowly add the oil. Transfer to a small glass or stainless steel bowl and season with the salt and pepper.

2. Prepare the grill for direct cooking over medium heat (350° to 450°F).

3. Brush the cooking grates clean. Lightly brush the squashes, pepper, and bread on all sides with oil and season evenly with salt and pepper. Grill over **direct medium heat**, with the lid closed as much as possible, until the vegetables are slightly charred and the bread has grill marks, turning once. The vegetables will take 4 to 6 minutes and the bread will take 2 to 4 minutes. Remove from the grill and let cool.

4. Coat the chicken on both sides with 3 tablespoons of the dressing. Grill, smooth (skin) side down first, over **direct medium heat**, with the lid closed as much as possible, until the meat is firm to the touch and opaque all the way to the center, 8 to 12 minutes, turning once or twice. Remove from the grill and let rest for 3 to 5 minutes.

5. Cut the vegetables, bread, and chicken into ½-inch cubes and combine in a large bowl with the tomatoes and feta. Add the dressing and toss to coat. Serve immediately.

SERVES: 4 to 6

TIP!
Cooking for a crowd?
This recipe doubles nicely.

66

CHICKEN AND APPLE SALAD
WITH CHEDDAR CHEESE AND CASHEWS

PREP TIME: 20 minutes
MARINATING TIME: 15 to 30 minutes
GRILLING TIME: 8 to 12 minutes

Dressing

¼ cup fresh lime juice
3 tablespoons honey
2 tablespoons minced shallot
1 tablespoon Dijon mustard
1 tablespoon minced fresh rosemary leaves
1 teaspoon kosher salt
½ teaspoon ground black pepper
⅓ cup extra-virgin olive oil

3 boneless, skinless chicken breast halves, about 6 ounces each
1 medium red onion, cut crosswise into ⅓-inch slices
1 romaine lettuce heart, cut crosswise into ½-inch strips
2 small red apples, cut into ¼-inch slices
1 cup green grapes
½ cup cashews
½ cup diced cheddar cheese

1. In a small glass or stainless steel bowl, whisk the dressing ingredients, except the oil. Slowly whisk in the oil to make a smooth dressing.

2. Prepare the grill for direct cooking over medium heat (350° to 450°F).

3. Place the chicken breasts in a large glass or stainless steel bowl and add ¼ cup of the dressing; turn to coat. Allow the chicken to marinate at room temperature for 15 to 30 minutes before grilling. Spoon 2 tablespoons of the dressing over the onion slices and gently turn to coat evenly.

4. Brush the cooking grates clean. Grill the chicken, smooth (skin) side down first, over **direct medium heat**, with the lid closed as much as possible, until the meat is firm to the touch and opaque all the way to the center, 8 to 12 minutes, turning once or twice. Grill the onion slices with the chicken over **direct medium heat** until charred in spots and tender, about 8 minutes, turning once. Remove the chicken and the onions from the grill and let the chicken rest for 3 to 5 minutes.

5. Combine the remaining ingredients in a large serving bowl. Cut the chicken into thin strips and roughly chop the onions. Add the chicken and onions to the bowl. Add enough of the remaining dressing to coat the ingredients lightly (you may not need all of it). Mix well. Serve at room temperature.

SERVES: 4 to 6

GRILLED CHICKEN SALAD NIÇOISE
WITH SHERRY VINAIGRETTE

PREP TIME: 35 minutes
GRILLING TIME: 8 to 12 minutes

Vinaigrette
- ¾ cup extra-virgin olive oil
- ¼ cup sherry vinegar
- 2 tablespoons minced shallot
- 1½ tablespoons finely chopped fresh marjoram leaves
- 1 tablespoon Dijon mustard
- ½ teaspoon kosher salt
- ¼ teaspoon ground black pepper

Salad
- 6 small red new potatoes, about 10 ounces total Kosher salt
- 6 ounces haricots verts (thin green beans), stems removed
- 4 boneless, skinless chicken breast halves, about 6 ounces each
- 1 small head butter lettuce, about 4 ounces, leaves separated
- 12 niçoise olives
- 12 small pear tomatoes, halved lengthwise, or 3 plum tomatoes, cut crosswise into ¼-inch-thick slices
- 4 hard-boiled eggs, quartered

1. In a small glass or stainless steel bowl, whisk the vinaigrette ingredients.

2. Prepare the grill for direct cooking over medium heat (350° to 450°F).

3. Fill a large saucepan three-quarters full with water and bring to a boil. Add the potatoes and boil until barely tender, about 10 minutes. Remove the potatoes with a slotted spoon and, when cool enough to handle, cut them in half. Return the water to a boil, add a teaspoon or two of salt, and then add the green beans. Boil until just crisp-tender, 2 to 3 minutes. Drain and cool under cold running water.

4. Place the potatoes and chicken breasts in a shallow glass dish. Pour ¼ cup of the vinaigrette over them and turn to coat well. Reserve the remaining vinaigrette to dress the salad.

5. Brush the cooking grates clean. Grill the potatoes and the chicken, smooth (skin) side down first, over **direct medium heat**, with the lid closed as much as possible, until the potatoes are golden brown and the meat is firm to the touch and opaque all the way to the center, 8 to 12 minutes, turning once or twice. Remove from the grill and let rest for 3 to 5 minutes. Cut the chicken crosswise into ¼-inch slices.

6. Arrange a few lettuce leaves on each plate with some olives and tomatoes. Place the eggs, green beans, and potatoes around the plate. Top with chicken slices. Drizzle the reserved vinaigrette over the salad. Serve at room temperature.

SERVES: 4

70

CHICKEN SOUVLAKI
WITH MINTY FETA DRESSING

PREP TIME: 40 minutes
GRILLING TIME: 6 to 8 minutes
SPECIAL EQUIPMENT: 8 metal or bamboo skewers (if using bamboo, soak in water for at least 30 minutes)

Marinade
- ½ cup roughly chopped fresh Italian parsley leaves
- ¼ cup dry white wine
- ¼ cup extra-virgin olive oil
  - Grated zest and juice from ½ lemon
- 1 teaspoon granulated garlic
- 1 teaspoon dried oregano
- 1 teaspoon paprika
- ¾ teaspoon kosher salt
- ¼ teaspoon ground black pepper

- 4 boneless, skinless chicken breast halves, about 6 ounces each

Salad
- 6 ounces romaine lettuce leaves, roughly chopped
- 2 medium ripe tomatoes, cut into wedges
- 1 yellow or orange bell pepper, stemmed, seeded, and cut into bite-sized pieces
- ½ English cucumber, cut into ½-inch chunks
- ½ cup pitted kalamata olives
- ⅓ cup slivered red onion

Dressing
- 3 ounces feta cheese, crumbled
- ¼ cup loosely packed fresh mint leaves
- 2 tablespoons extra-virgin olive oil
- 1 tablespoon white wine vinegar
- 1 small garlic clove, roughly chopped

1. In a large glass or stainless steel bowl, whisk the marinade ingredients. Cut the chicken lengthwise into even strips, each about 1 to 1½ inches thick. Cut the strips crosswise into 1- to 1½-inch pieces. Add the chicken to the bowl with the marinade and mix well. Cover and refrigerate until needed.

2. In a large bowl combine the salad ingredients. Cover and refrigerate until just before serving.

3. In a blender or food processor, combine the dressing ingredients, including 2 tablespoons of water. Blend until thick and smooth, scraping down the sides as needed. Season with salt and pepper.

4. Prepare the grill for direct cooking over high heat (450° to 550°F).

5. Thread the chicken pieces onto skewers. Discard any leftover marinade. Lightly coat the chicken pieces with oil.

6. Brush the cooking grates clean. Grill the skewers over **direct high heat**, with the lid closed as much as possible, until the meat is firm to the touch and opaque all the way to the center, 6 to 8 minutes, turning once or twice.

7. Just before serving, add enough of the dressing to coat the salad ingredients lightly. Mix well.

8. Remove the chicken from the skewers while still warm and place on top of the salad. Season with salt and pepper. Serve any remaining dressing on the side.

SERVES: 4 to 6

CHICKEN COBB SALAD
AND LEMON-MUSTARD DRESSING

PREP TIME: 40 minutes
GRILLING TIME: 12 to 16 minutes

Dressing

- 3 tablespoons red wine vinegar
- 1½ tablespoons minced shallot
- 2 teaspoons fresh lemon juice
- 1 tablespoon Dijon mustard
- ⅔ cup extra-virgin olive oil
  Kosher salt
  Ground black pepper

- 3 boneless, skinless chicken breast halves, about 6 ounces each
- 3 romaine lettuce hearts, about 1½ pounds, quartered through their cores
- 2 medium tomatoes, cut into wedges
- ½ English cucumber, cut into ½-inch cubes
- 1 medium Hass avocado, cut into ½-inch cubes
- 8 slices bacon, cooked, crumbled
- 4 hard-boiled eggs, quartered
- 4 ounces blue cheese, crumbled

1. In a small stainless steel or glass bowl, whisk the vinegar, shallot, lemon juice, and mustard. Slowly whisk in the oil until it is emulsified. Season with salt and pepper.

2. Prepare the grill for direct cooking over medium heat (350° to 450°F).

3. Place the chicken breasts in a large stainless steel or glass bowl. Add 3 tablespoons of the dressing and turn to coat evenly. Cover and refrigerate until ready to grill.

4. Place the romaine on a large rimmed sheet pan. Drizzle ¼ cup of the dressing on the lettuce and turn to coat evenly. Season with salt and pepper.

5. Brush the cooking grates clean. Grill the chicken, smooth (skin) side down first, over ***direct medium heat***, with the lid closed as much as possible, until the meat is firm to the touch and opaque all the way to the center, 8 to 12 minutes, turning once or twice. Remove the chicken from the grill and let rest while you grill the lettuce.

6. Grill the lettuce over ***direct medium heat***, with the lid closed as much as possible, until charred in spots, about 4 minutes, turning occasionally.

7. Cut the chicken into ½-inch cubes. Divide the chicken, lettuce, tomatoes, cucumber, avocado, bacon, and eggs evenly among four plates. Spoon dressing over each salad and finish with the cheese.

SERVES: 4

VIETNAMESE CHICKEN SALAD
WITH LIME AND SESAME DRESSING

PREP TIME: 25 minutes
MARINATING TIME: 1 to 4 hours
GRILLING TIME: 4 to 6 minutes

Marinade

- ½ cup peanut oil
- ¼ cup fresh lime juice
- 2 tablespoons fish sauce
- 2 tablespoons granulated sugar
- 1 tablespoon rice vinegar
- 1 teaspoon toasted sesame oil
- ½ teaspoon kosher salt
- ½ teaspoon crushed red pepper flakes
- ¼ teaspoon ground black pepper

- 4 boneless, skinless chicken breast halves (without tenders), 4 to 6 ounces each

Salad

- 4 heaping cups shredded savoy or napa cabbage
- 1 cup shredded carrots
- ½ cup whole fresh mint leaves
- ¼ cup whole fresh basil leaves (torn if large)
- 2 scallions (white and light green parts only), very thinly sliced on the bias

- ½ cup finely chopped roasted, salted peanuts

1. In a medium glass or stainless steel bowl, whisk the marinade ingredients.

2. One at a time, place each breast, smooth side down, between two sheets of plastic wrap and pound to an even ½-inch thickness.

3. Place the chicken in a large, resealable plastic bag and pour in half of the marinade. Reserve the other half to use as a dressing for the salad. Press the air out of the bag and seal tightly. Turn the bag to distribute the marinade, place in a bowl, and refrigerate for 1 to 4 hours, turning occasionally.

4. Prepare the grill for direct cooking over high heat (450° to 550°F).

5. Remove the chicken from the bag and discard the marinade.

6. Brush the cooking grates clean. Grill the chicken, smooth (skin) side down first, over **direct high heat**, with the lid closed as much as possible, until the meat is firm to the touch and opaque all the way to the center, 4 to 6 minutes, turning once or twice. Transfer to a cutting board and let rest for 3 to 5 minutes. Cut on the bias into ¼-inch-thick slices.

7. In a large bowl mix the salad ingredients. Whisk the reserved dressing and pour some of it over the salad. Divide the salad evenly among four plates, and then add the chicken. Drizzle any juices that remain on the cutting board over the sliced chicken. Top with the peanuts and serve right away.

SERVES: 4

FARFALLE SALAD
WITH GRILLED CHICKEN AND SUMMER VEGETABLES

PREP TIME: 30 minutes, plus time to cook the pasta
GRILLING TIME: 8 to 12 minutes

Dressing
- ½ cup extra-virgin olive oil
- ¼ cup red wine vinegar
- ¼ cup roughly chopped fresh basil leaves
- 2 teaspoons whole-grain mustard
- 1 teaspoon granulated garlic
- 1 teaspoon kosher salt
- ½ teaspoon ground black pepper

- 3 boneless, skinless chicken breast halves (without tenders), 4 to 6 ounces each
- 2 small zucchini squashes, cut in half lengthwise
- 4 ripe plum tomatoes, cut in half lengthwise
- 1 large red onion, cut crosswise into ½-inch slices
- 8 ounces farfalle (bow tie) pasta
  Kosher salt
  Ground black pepper
- ⅓ cup freshly grated Parmigiano-Reggiano® cheese

1. Prepare the grill for direct cooking over medium heat (350° to 450°F).

2. In a medium glass or stainless steel bowl, whisk the dressing ingredients. Set aside 3 tablespoons of the dressing to brush on the raw chicken.

3. One at a time, place each breast, smooth side down, between two sheets of plastic wrap and pound to an even ½-inch thickness. Lightly brush the chicken on both sides with the reserved dressing.

4. Brush the vegetables all over with some of the dressing remaining in the medium bowl.

5. Brush the cooking grates clean. Grill the chicken, smooth (skin) side down first, over *direct medium heat*, with the lid closed as much as possible, until opaque all the way to the center, 6 to 8 minutes, turning once or twice. At the same time, grill the vegetables over *direct medium heat* until tender, turning once or twice. The zucchini will take 4 to 6 minutes, the tomatoes will take 6 to 8 minutes, and the onion will take 8 to 12 minutes.

6. Cook the pasta according to package directions. Drain the pasta and put it into a large serving bowl. Whisk the remaining dressing and add enough to coat the pasta lightly.

7. Cut the chicken and vegetables into bite-sized pieces. Add them to the bowl along with a little more dressing. Mix well. Season with salt and pepper. Serve warm with the cheese on the side.

SERVES: 6

MALAYSIAN CHICKEN SALAD
WITH CUCUMBERS, CARROTS, AND PEANUT DRESSING

PREP TIME: 30 minutes
MARINATING TIME: 1 to 2 hours
GRILLING TIME: 8 to 10 minutes

Marinade

- 2 tablespoons vegetable oil
- 2 tablespoons minced fresh ginger
- 1 tablespoon minced garlic
- 1 can (13.5 ounces) unsweetened coconut milk
- ⅓ cup smooth peanut butter
- ⅓ cup low-sodium soy sauce
- 3 tablespoons fresh lime juice
- 1 tablespoon brown sugar
- ¼ teaspoon pure chile powder

- 4 boneless, skinless chicken breast halves (without tenders), 4 to 6 ounces each

Salad

- 1 medium head butter lettuce, coarsely chopped
- 1 six-inch piece English cucumber, halved lengthwise and cut into thin half-moons
- ½ cup shredded carrot
- 1 large mango or papaya, seeded and cut into ½-inch cubes
- ⅓ cup coarsely chopped honey-roasted peanuts
- ¼ cup coarsely chopped fresh mint leaves
- 2 limes, cut in half (optional)

1. In a small saucepan over low heat, combine the oil, ginger, and garlic; sauté for about 2 minutes. Add the remaining marinade ingredients and whisk until smooth. Cook over low heat until the mixture comes to a simmer.

2. Pour half of the marinade into a large stainless steel or glass bowl, and let cool to room temperature. Set the other half aside at room temperature to use as a dressing for the salad.

3. Add the chicken breasts to the marinade and turn to coat evenly. Cover and refrigerate for 1 to 2 hours.

4. Prepare the grill for direct cooking over medium heat (350° to 450°F).

5. Brush the cooking grates clean. Remove the chicken from the bowl and wipe off most of the marinade. Discard the marinade. Grill the chicken, smooth (skin) side down first, over ***direct medium heat***, with the lid closed as much as possible, until the meat is firm to the touch and opaque all the way to the center, 8 to 10 minutes, turning once or twice. Remove from the grill and let rest for 3 to 5 minutes.

6. Cut the chicken crosswise into thin slices. Arrange the lettuce, cucumber, carrot, mango, and chicken evenly on four plates. Reheat the reserved dressing over low heat, whisk until smooth, and drizzle some of it over the salad (you may not need all of the dressing). Garnish with peanuts and mint. If desired, squeeze a little lime juice over the top. Serve warm.

SERVES: 4

HONEY-MUSTARD CHICKEN SANDWICHES
WITH AVOCADO AND ARUGULA

PREP TIME: 20 minutes
MARINATING TIME: 1 to 2 hours
GRILLING TIME: 8 to 12 minutes

Marinade

- ¼ cup extra-virgin olive oil
- 2 tablespoons cider vinegar
- 1 tablespoon Dijon mustard
- 1 tablespoon honey
- 1 teaspoon kosher salt

- 4 boneless, skinless chicken breast halves, about 6 ounces each
- 8 slices sourdough bread
- ¼ cup bottled blue cheese dressing
- 4 teaspoons Dijon mustard
- 1 ripe Hass avocado, cut into ¼-inch slices
- 1 cup loosely packed baby arugula
- 1 medium ripe tomato, cut into ⅛-inch slices

1. In a small bowl whisk the marinade ingredients. Place the chicken in a large, resealable plastic bag and pour in the marinade. Press the air out of the bag and seal tightly. Turn the bag several times to distribute the marinade, and refrigerate for 1 to 2 hours.

2. Prepare the grill for direct cooking over medium heat (350° to 450°F).

3. Brush the cooking grates clean. Remove the chicken from the bag and discard the marinade. Grill the chicken, smooth (skin) side down first, over *direct medium heat*, with the lid closed as much as possible, until the meat is firm to the touch and opaque all the way to the center, 8 to 12 minutes, turning once or twice. During the last minute of grilling time, lightly toast the bread over *direct medium heat*, turning once. Remove from the grill and let the chicken rest for 3 to 5 minutes. Cut the chicken crosswise into ½-inch slices.

4. Spread the blue cheese dressing and mustard on one side of each slice of bread. Build the sandwiches with the avocado and chicken slices on the bottom, followed by the arugula and tomato slices. Cover with the remaining slices of bread and serve warm or at room temperature.

SERVES: 4

CHICKEN SANDWICHES
WITH PICKLED PEPPERS AND CREAMY LEMON SPREAD

PREP TIME: 20 minutes
GRILLING TIME: 6 to 8 minutes

Rub

- 1 teaspoon celery seed
- 1 teaspoon granulated garlic
- 1 teaspoon kosher salt
- ½ teaspoon ground black pepper

- 4 boneless, skinless chicken breast halves (without tenders), 4 to 6 ounces each
  Extra-virgin olive oil
- ½ cup mayonnaise
- 1 tablespoon fresh lemon juice
- 4 sourdough rolls, each about 6 inches long, halved lengthwise
- 8 lettuce leaves
- ½ cup pepperoncini, drained, stemmed, and roughly chopped

1. Prepare the grill for direct cooking over medium heat (350° to 450°F).

2. In a small bowl mix the rub ingredients.

3. One at a time, place each chicken breast, smooth side down, between two sheets of plastic wrap and pound to an even ½-inch thickness. Each breast should be about the same length and width as the sourdough rolls.

4. Lightly coat the chicken on both sides with oil. Use 2¼ teaspoons of the rub to season the chicken evenly.

5. In a small glass or stainless steel bowl, mix the mayonnaise, lemon juice, and the remaining 1¼ teaspoons of the rub.

6. Brush the cooking grates clean. Grill the chicken, smooth (skin) side down first, over *direct medium heat*, with the lid closed as much as possible, until the meat is firm to the touch and opaque all the way to the center, 6 to 8 minutes, turning once or twice. During the last 30 seconds of grilling time, toast the rolls, cut sides down, over *direct medium heat*.

7. Spread the mayonnaise mixture on the inside of the rolls. Build the sandwiches with the chicken, lettuce, and pepperoncini. Serve warm.

SERVES: 4

CHICKEN CORDON BLEU PANINI
WITH HAM AND SWISS CHEESE

PREP TIME: 15 minutes
MARINATING TIME: 20 to 30 minutes
GRILLING TIME: 14 to 20 minutes
SPECIAL EQUIPMENT: sheet pan and
2 foil-wrapped bricks or cast-iron skillet

Marinade

2 tablespoons extra-virgin olive oil
1 tablespoon Dijon mustard
1 teaspoon minced garlic
½ teaspoon kosher salt
¼ teaspoon ground black pepper

2 boneless, skinless chicken breast halves,
6 to 8 ounces each

Dijon mustard
8 slices crusty sourdough bread, each ½ inch thick
8 thin slices deli ham, about 8 ounces total
8 thin slices Swiss cheese, about 8 ounces total
Extra-virgin olive oil

1. Prepare the grill for direct cooking over medium heat (350° to 450°F).

2. In a medium bowl whisk the marinade ingredients. Add the chicken to the bowl and turn to coat evenly. Allow the chicken to marinate at room temperature for 20 to 30 minutes.

3. Remove the chicken from the bowl and discard the marinade. Brush the cooking grates clean. Grill the chicken, smooth (skin) side down first, over *direct medium heat*, with the lid closed as much as possible, until the meat is firm to the touch and opaque all the way to the center, 8 to 12 minutes, turning once or twice. Remove from the grill and let rest for 3 to 5 minutes. Cut the chicken into ½-inch strips.

4. Reduce the temperature of the grill to low heat (250° to 350°F).

5. Lightly spread mustard on one side of 4 slices of bread. Top with 2 slices of ham and 2 slices of cheese. Layer each sandwich with chicken strips and top with the remaining bread slices. Lightly brush each sandwich on both sides with oil, and press down on each sandwich so it is compacted. Brush the cooking grates clean. Place the sandwiches over *direct low heat* and put a sheet pan with 2 foil-wrapped bricks (or use a cast-iron skillet) directly on top of the sandwiches. Grill, uncovered, for 3 to 4 minutes. Carefully remove the weight, turn the sandwiches over, replace the weight, and grill until the bread is toasted and the cheese has melted, 3 to 4 minutes more. Remove from the grill and serve right away.

SERVES: 4

LEMON-DILL CHICKEN WRAPS
WITH GRATED CARROTS

PREP TIME: 20 minutes
GRILLING TIME: 8 to 12 minutes

Dressing
½ cup mayonnaise
2 tablespoons finely chopped fresh dill
2 teaspoons fresh lemon juice
½ teaspoon kosher salt
¼ teaspoon ground black pepper

4 boneless, skinless chicken breast halves,
   about 6 ounces each
3 tablespoons extra-virgin olive oil
½ teaspoon kosher salt
¼ teaspoon ground black pepper

4 large spinach flour tortillas (10 inches)
1⅓ cups grated carrots

1. Prepare the grill for direct cooking over medium heat (350° to 450°F).

2. In a large glass or stainless steel bowl, whisk the dressing ingredients.

3. Brush the chicken on both sides with the oil and season evenly with the salt and pepper.

4. Brush the cooking grates clean. Grill the chicken, smooth (skin) side down first, over **direct medium heat**, with the lid closed as much as possible, until the meat is firm to the touch and opaque all the way to the center, 8 to 12 minutes, turning once or twice. Remove from the grill and let rest for 3 to 5 minutes.

5. Quarter each piece of chicken lengthwise, and then cut crosswise into very thin slices. Add the chicken to the dressing and mix well to coat all the slices.

6. Lay the tortillas in a single layer on a work surface. Evenly divide the chicken mixture, and then the carrots, over three-quarters of each tortilla, leaving one-quarter of the tortilla empty at the top. Roll up each tortilla like a jelly roll. Trim off any uneven ends. Cut the rolls into equal pieces, each about 1 inch thick. Arrange, cut sides up, on a platter. Serve at room temperature.

SERVES: 4

PAPRIKA CHICKEN
WITH ROMESCO SAUCE

PREP TIME: 20 minutes
GRILLING TIME: 20 to 27 minutes

Sauce

- 2 medium red bell peppers
- ¼ cup whole almonds
- 1 medium garlic clove
- ½ cup loosely packed fresh Italian parsley leaves and tender stems
- 2 teaspoons sherry vinegar
- ½ teaspoon kosher salt
- ⅛ teaspoon ground cayenne pepper
- ¼ cup extra-virgin olive oil

Rub

- 1 teaspoon paprika
- 1 teaspoon granulated onion
- ¾ teaspoon kosher salt
- ½ teaspoon ground black pepper
- ¼ teaspoon ground cayenne pepper

- 4 boneless, skinless chicken breast halves, about 6 ounces each
  Extra-virgin olive oil

1. Prepare the grill for direct cooking over medium heat (350° to 450°F).

2. Brush the cooking grates clean. Grill the bell peppers over **direct medium heat**, with the lid closed as much as possible, until they are blackened and blistered all over, 12 to 15 minutes, turning occasionally. Place the peppers in a medium bowl and cover with plastic wrap to trap the steam. Set aside for at least 10 minutes. Remove the peppers from the bowl and peel away and discard the skin, cut off and discard the stems and seeds, and then roughly chop the peppers.

3. In a small skillet over medium heat, toast the almonds until their aroma is apparent, 3 to 5 minutes, stirring occasionally. In a food processor finely chop the almonds and garlic. Add the peppers, parsley, vinegar, salt, and cayenne. Process to create a coarse paste. With the motor running, slowly add the oil and process to create a fairly smooth sauce.

4. In a small bowl combine the rub ingredients. Lightly brush the chicken on both sides with oil and season evenly with the rub.

5. Grill the chicken, smooth (skin) side down first, over **direct medium heat**, with the lid closed as much as possible, until the meat is firm to the touch and opaque all the way to the center, 8 to 12 minutes, turning once or twice. Remove from the grill and let rest for 3 to 5 minutes. Serve warm with the sauce.

SERVES: 4

GRILLED CHICKEN TACOS
WITH LIME-CILANTRO SLAW

PREP TIME: 30 minutes
MARINATING TIME: 1 to 2 hours
GRILLING TIME: 8 to 12 minutes

Marinade

- 2 tablespoons extra-virgin olive oil
- 2 tablespoons fresh lime juice
- 1 teaspoon prepared chili powder
- ½ teaspoon kosher salt
- ¼ teaspoon ground black pepper

- 4 boneless, skinless chicken breast halves, about 6 ounces each

Slaw

- ¼ cup extra-virgin olive oil
- ¼ cup fresh lime juice
- ¾ teaspoon kosher salt
- 6 cups finely shredded green cabbage
- 1 cup roughly chopped fresh cilantro leaves
- ½ cup thinly sliced scallions (white and light green parts only)
- 1 teaspoon ground cumin

- ½ cup sour cream
- 1 teaspoon finely chopped canned chipotle chiles in adobo
  Kosher salt
- 8 corn or flour tortillas (6 to 7 inches)
- 1 cup tomato salsa

1. In a large glass or stainless steel bowl, whisk the marinade ingredients. Add the chicken to the bowl and turn to coat evenly. Cover and refrigerate for 1 to 2 hours.

2. In a large glass or stainless steel bowl, whisk the oil, lime juice, and salt. Add the remaining slaw ingredients and mix well.

3. In a small bowl whisk the sour cream and chile. Season with salt and more chile, if desired. Refrigerate the slaw and sauce until ready to serve.

4. Evenly divide the tortillas into 2 foil packets.

5. Prepare the grill for direct cooking over medium heat (350° to 450°F).

6. Brush the cooking grates clean. Remove the chicken from the bowl and discard the marinade. Grill the chicken, smooth (skin) side down first, over **direct medium heat**, with the lid closed as much as possible, until the meat is firm to the touch and opaque all the way to the center, 8 to 12 minutes, turning once or twice. During the last 2 to 3 minutes of grilling time, heat the tortilla packets over **direct medium heat**, turning once. Remove the chicken and tortillas from the grill and let the chicken rest for 3 to 5 minutes. Cut the chicken crosswise into thin slices.

7. To assemble the tacos, divide the chicken slices evenly among the tortillas. Top with the slaw, some salsa, and a dollop of sauce. Fold in half and serve immediately.

SERVES: 4 to 6

MEXICAN CHICKEN BOWL
WITH RICE, BEANS, AND QUESO FRESCO

PREP TIME: 20 minutes, plus 20 minutes for the rice
GRILLING TIME: 8 to 12 minutes

Marinade
- 2 canned chipotle chiles in adobo, minced
- 2 tablespoons extra-virgin olive oil
- 2 tablespoons fresh lime juice
- 1 tablespoon ancho chile powder
- 1 tablespoon minced garlic
- 2 teaspoons ground cumin
- 1 teaspoon kosher salt
- ¼ teaspoon ground black pepper

- 3 boneless, skinless chicken breast halves, about 6 ounces each

Rice
- 1½ cups long-grain white rice
- 3 cups low-sodium chicken broth
- ½ teaspoon kosher salt
- ¼ cup finely chopped fresh cilantro leaves
- 2 tablespoons fresh lime juice

- 2 medium Hass avocados, cut into ½-inch dice
- 2 medium tomatoes, cut into ½-inch dice
- ½ cup finely chopped red onion, rinsed in a sieve under cold water
- 1 can (15 ounces) pinto beans, rinsed
- 1 cup crumbled queso fresco
- 2 limes, cut into wedges
- 6 handfuls tortilla chips

1. In a small bowl whisk the marinade ingredients. Place the chicken in a large, resealable plastic bag and pour in the marinade. Press the air out of the bag and seal tightly. Turn the bag to distribute the marinade, and refrigerate while you prepare the rice.

2. In a medium saucepan over medium heat, bring the rice, broth, and salt to a simmer. Reduce the heat to low and cook, covered, until the rice is tender and the liquid is absorbed, about 20 minutes. Move off the burner and keep covered for 10 minutes. Stir in the cilantro and lime juice. Keep a lid on the rice until ready to use.

3. While the rice is cooking, prepare the grill for direct cooking over medium heat (350° to 450°F).

4. Brush the cooking grates clean. Remove the chicken from the bag and discard the marinade. Grill the chicken, smooth (skin) side down first, over *direct medium heat*, with the lid closed as much as possible, until the meat is firm to the touch and opaque all the way to the center, 8 to 12 minutes, turning once or twice. Transfer the chicken to a cutting board and let rest for 3 to 5 minutes. Cut into ½-inch chunks.

5. Divide the rice evenly among individual bowls. Top the rice with small mounds of chicken, avocado, tomato, onion, and beans. Sprinkle the queso fresco on top. Serve with lime wedges and tortilla chips.

SERVES: 4 to 6

BARBECUED CHICKEN PIZZA
WITH SMOKED MOZZARELLA

PREP TIME: 25 minutes
GRILLING TIME: 16 to 32 minutes

4 boneless, skinless chicken breast halves,
about 6 ounces each
Extra-virgin olive oil
1½ teaspoons kosher salt
½ teaspoon ground black pepper
½ cup barbecue sauce
2 pounds homemade or store-bought pizza dough
1 cup tomato or marinara sauce
2 cups (8 ounces) grated smoked
mozzarella cheese
¼ cup roughly chopped fresh basil leaves
Crushed red pepper flakes

1. Prepare the grill for direct cooking over medium heat (350° to 450°F).

2. Lightly coat the chicken on both sides with oil and season evenly with the salt and pepper. Brush the cooking grates clean. Grill the chicken, smooth (skin) side down first, over *direct medium heat*, with the lid closed as much as possible, until the meat is firm to the touch and opaque all the way to the center, 8 to 12 minutes, turning once or twice. Remove from the grill and roughly chop. Moisten with the barbecue sauce.

3. Cut the dough into 4 pieces. Lightly brush four 12-inch squares of parchment paper on one side with oil. Flatten each piece of dough on a sheet of parchment to create 4 rounds. Each round should be about ¼ inch thick and 8 to 10 inches in diameter. Lightly brush the tops with oil. Let the rounds sit at room temperature for 5 to 10 minutes.

4. Place 2 rounds on the cooking grate with the paper sides facing up. Grill over *direct medium heat*, with the lid closed as much as possible, until the dough is well marked on the underside, 2 to 5 minutes. Peel off and discard the parchment paper. Transfer the crusts to a work surface with the grilled sides facing up. Repeat with the other 2 rounds.

5. Spread the tomato sauce over the crusts, and then add the chicken and cheese. Grill over *direct medium heat* until the cheese is melted and the bottoms are crisp, 2 to 5 minutes, rotating the pizzas for even cooking. Remove from the grill and add the basil and pepper flakes. Cut into wedges and serve warm.

SERVES: 4

KICK'N CHICKEN BREASTS
WITH YOGURT-CUCUMBER SAUCE

PREP TIME: 10 minutes
GRILLING TIME: 8 to 12 minutes

Sauce
- ¾ cup plain yogurt
- ⅓ cup coarsely grated English cucumber
- 1 teaspoon Weber® Kick'n Chicken® Seasoning

- 4 boneless, skinless chicken breast halves, about 6 ounces each
  Extra-virgin olive oil
- 1 tablespoon Weber® Kick'n Chicken® Seasoning
- 16 very thin slices English cucumber, cut in half crosswise

1. Prepare the grill for direct cooking over medium heat (350° to 450°F).

2. In a small bowl combine the sauce ingredients.

3. Lightly coat the chicken on both sides with oil and sprinkle evenly with the seasoning. Brush the cooking grates clean. Grill the chicken, smooth (skin) side down first, over *direct medium heat*, with the lid closed as much as possible, until the meat is firm to the touch and opaque all the way to the center, 8 to 12 minutes, turning once or twice. Remove from the grill and let rest for 3 to 5 minutes. Serve warm with the sauce and cucumber slices.

SERVES: 4

CUMIN-CORIANDER CHICKEN BREASTS
WITH PUMPKIN SEED PESTO

PREP TIME: 15 minutes
GRILL TIME: 8 to 12 minutes
SPECIAL EQUIPMENT: spice mill

Pesto

1 cup loosely packed fresh cilantro leaves and tender stems
½ cup loosely packed fresh Italian parsley leaves and tender stems
¼ cup raw shelled pumpkin seeds (pepitas)
1 garlic clove
2 tablespoons fresh orange juice
½ cup extra-virgin olive oil
 Kosher salt
 Ground black pepper

Rub

1 tablespoon coriander seed
2 teaspoons cumin seed
½ teaspoon kosher salt
¼ teaspoon ground black pepper

6 boneless, skinless chicken breast halves, about 6 ounces each
 Extra-virgin olive oil

1. In a food processor or blender, combine the cilantro, parsley, pumpkin seeds, garlic, and orange juice. Pulse until coarsely chopped, occasionally scraping down the sides of the bowl. With the machine running, slowly add the oil to create a smooth puree. Season with salt and pepper.

2. Prepare the grill for direct cooking over medium heat (350° to 450°F).

3. In a small skillet over medium heat, toast the coriander and cumin seeds until aromatic and slightly darker in color, 2 to 3 minutes, stirring often. Let cool, and then finely grind the seeds in a spice mill. Pour into a small bowl and mix with the salt and pepper.

4. Lightly brush the chicken on both sides with oil and season evenly with the rub.

5. Brush the cooking grates clean. Grill the chicken, smooth (skin) side down first, over ***direct medium heat***, with the lid closed as much as possible, until the meat is firm to the touch and opaque all the way to the center, 8 to 12 minutes, turning once or twice. Remove from the grill and let rest for 3 to 5 minutes. Serve warm with the pesto. Serving suggestion: Grilled Carrots (for recipe, see page 117).

SERVES: 6

MARINATED CHICKEN BREASTS
WITH TANGERINE SALSA

PREP TIME: 30 minutes
MARINATING TIME: 20 to 30 minutes
GRILLING TIME: 8 to 12 minutes

4   medium tangerines or clementines
3   tablespoons extra-virgin olive oil, divided
2   tablespoons plus 2 teaspoons fresh lime
    juice, divided
4   boneless, skinless chicken breast halves,
    about 6 ounces each
2   medium Hass avocados, finely diced
2   tablespoons roughly chopped fresh cilantro
    or basil leaves
1   large scallion (white and light green parts only),
    thinly sliced
    Kosher salt
    Ground black pepper

1. In a large glass or stainless steel bowl, combine the juice from 2 tangerines (you should have about ¼ cup), 2 tablespoons of the oil, and 2 tablespoons of the lime juice. Add the chicken and turn to coat evenly. Cover and marinate at room temperature for 20 to 30 minutes.

2. Prepare the grill for direct cooking over medium heat (350° to 450°F).

3. Peel and section the remaining tangerines. Cut the sections crosswise into thirds and place them in a medium glass or stainless steel bowl. Add the remaining 1 tablespoon of oil, the remaining 2 teaspoons of lime juice, the avocados, cilantro, and sliced scallion. Gently toss to combine, and season with salt and pepper.

4. Remove the chicken from the bowl and discard the marinade. Season the chicken evenly with ¾ teaspoon salt and ½ teaspoon pepper.

5. Brush the cooking grates clean. Grill the chicken, smooth (skin) side down first, over ***direct medium heat***, with the lid closed as much as possible, until the meat is firm to the touch and opaque all the way to the center, 8 to 12 minutes, turning once or twice. Remove from the grill and let rest for 3 to 5 minutes. Cut the chicken crosswise into ½-inch-thick slices. Spoon the salsa over the top and serve warm. Serving suggestion: Couscous Salad (for recipe, see page 125).

SERVES: 4

CHILE-RUBBED CHICKEN
WITH JICAMA, AVOCADO, AND ORANGE SALSA

PREP TIME: 1 hour
GRILLING TIME: 8 to 12 minutes

Salsa
1½ cups peeled and finely diced jicama
1 medium ripe Hass avocado, diced
¾ cup finely diced red onion, rinsed in a sieve
under cold water
½ cup finely diced red bell pepper
2 oranges, segmented, segments halved
1 teaspoon minced jalapeño chile pepper
¼ cup fresh lime juice
¼ teaspoon kosher salt

Rub
2 tablespoons pure chile powder
1 teaspoon kosher salt
¼ teaspoon ground black pepper

4 boneless, skinless chicken breast halves,
about 6 ounces each
1 tablespoon extra-virgin olive oil

NOTE
Raw onions can taste a little harsh in a salsa, but a good rinse under cold water will take the edge off.

1. In a medium glass or stainless steel bowl, combine the salsa ingredients.

2. Prepare the grill for direct cooking over medium heat (350° to 450°F).

3. In a small bowl combine the rub ingredients. Lightly brush the chicken on both sides with the oil and season evenly with the rub.

4. Brush the cooking grates clean. Grill the chicken, smooth (skin) side down first, over ***direct medium heat***, with the lid closed as much as possible, until the meat is firm to the touch and opaque all the way to the center, 8 to 12 minutes, turning once or twice. Remove from the grill and let rest for 3 to 5 minutes. Serve warm with the salsa. Serving suggestion: Red Chile Rice (for recipe, see page 120).

SERVES: 4

Who said every salsa needs tomatoes? The sweet, crunchy interior of jicama is a refreshing alternative when you mix it with other tropical ingredients like orange and avocado.

CHICKEN SALTIMBOCCA
IN WHITE WINE-BUTTER SAUCE

PREP TIME: 15 minutes, plus about 20 minutes for the sauce
GRILLING TIME: 6 to 8 minutes

    4   boneless, skinless chicken breast halves
        (without tenders), 4 to 6 ounces each
    ¾   teaspoon kosher salt
    ½   teaspoon ground black pepper
    8   whole fresh sage leaves
    8   thin slices prosciutto
        Extra-virgin olive oil

Sauce
    3   tablespoons unsalted butter
    2   tablespoons minced shallot
    ¼   cup dry white wine
    1   cup low-sodium chicken broth
    2   tablespoons fresh lemon juice
    2   tablespoons unsalted butter, cold
        Kosher salt
        Ground black pepper

1. Prepare the grill for direct cooking over medium heat (350° to 450°F).

2. One at a time, place each breast, smooth side down, between two sheets of plastic wrap and pound to an even ½-inch thickness.

3. Season the chicken on both sides with the salt and pepper. Place the chicken, smooth side down, on a work surface. Lay 2 sage leaves on top of each piece of chicken. Then wrap 2 slices of prosciutto around each breast, staggering them slightly so the meat is completely covered and the ends meet on the other side. Press the prosciutto so that it clings to the chicken. Lightly brush both sides with oil.

The prosciutto and sage that you wrap around each chicken breast will flavor the meat during grilling.

4. In a medium skillet over medium-high heat, melt 3 tablespoons of butter. Add the shallot and cook until it just turns tender, 3 to 4 minutes, stirring occasionally. Add the wine and bring to a simmer. Add the chicken broth and lemon juice. Bring to a boil and reduce by half, about 10 minutes, stirring occasionally. The sauce should barely coat the back of a spoon. Remove the sauce from the heat and blend in the cold butter, 1 tablespoon at a time. Season with salt and pepper and set aside.

5. Brush the cooking grates clean. Grill the chicken, sage side down, over *direct medium heat*, with the lid closed as much as possible, for 3 to 4 minutes. Using a metal spatula, gently turn the chicken over, taking care not to tear the prosciutto. Grill for 3 to 4 minutes more. To check for doneness, cut into the underside of one breast. The meat should be opaque all the way to the center. Remove from the grill and let rest for 3 to 5 minutes. Warm the sauce over medium heat.

6. Serve the chicken warm with the sauce.

SERVES: 4

PROSCIUTTO-WRAPPED CHICKEN
WITH FIG-BALSAMIC GLAZE

PREP TIME: 10 minutes, plus about 15 minutes
for the glaze
GRILLING TIME: 6 to 8 minutes

Glaze

- ¼ cup balsamic vinegar
- 2 dried figs, finely chopped
- 2 tablespoons minced shallot
- 1 tablespoon honey
- 1 tablespoon fresh lemon juice

- 4 boneless, skinless chicken breast halves
  (without tenders), 4 to 6 ounces each
  Kosher salt
  Ground black pepper
- 4 thin slices prosciutto
- 8 fresh figs, about 1¼ ounces each, stems
  removed, cut in half lengthwise
  Extra-virgin olive oil
- 4 cups baby arugula
- ½ cup thinly shaved Parmigiano-Reggiano® cheese

1. In a small saucepan over medium heat, combine the vinegar, dried figs, and shallot. Bring to a boil, reduce the heat to low, and simmer until almost all of the liquid has reduced to a thick, syrupy consistency, about 10 minutes. Remove from the heat and stir in the honey and lemon juice. Pour the glaze through a fine mesh strainer into a glass or stainless steel bowl, and discard the pulp. Set aside to cool.

2. One at a time, place each breast, smooth side down, between two sheets of plastic wrap and pound to an even ½-inch thickness. Season both sides of the chicken with salt and pepper. Wrap one piece of prosciutto around the center of each breast, pressing the loose ends of the prosciutto down so the meat stays together. Lightly brush the chicken on both sides and the cut sides of the figs with oil.

The concentrated intensity of dried figs (left) works best for the glaze here, but for grilling you will appreciate the plumpness and juiciness of fresh figs.

3. Prepare the grill for direct cooking over medium heat (350° to 450°F).

4. Brush the cooking grates clean. Grill the chicken, smooth (skin) side down first, over *direct medium heat*, with the lid closed as much as possible, until the meat is firm to the touch and opaque all the way to the center, 6 to 8 minutes, turning once or twice. At the same time, grill the figs over *direct medium heat* until well marked and heated through, about 4 minutes, turning once after 3 minutes.

5. Divide the arugula evenly among four plates. Place one chicken breast on each serving of arugula along with 4 fig halves. Drizzle the chicken and arugula with the glaze and top with the cheese.

SERVES: 4

CHICKEN SKEWERS
MARINATED IN BASIL AND SUN-DRIED TOMATOES

PREP TIME: 15 minutes
MARINATING TIME: 2 to 3 hours
GRILLING TIME: 6 to 8 minutes
SPECIAL EQUIPMENT: 8 to 12 metal or bamboo skewers (if using bamboo, soak in water for at least 30 minutes)

Paste
1 cup loosely packed fresh basil leaves
¼ cup oil-packed sun-dried tomatoes
3 garlic cloves
1 teaspoon kosher salt
½ teaspoon ground black pepper
½ teaspoon dried oregano
6 tablespoons extra-virgin olive oil
2 tablespoons red wine vinegar

4 boneless, skinless chicken breast halves, about 6 ounces each

1. In the bowl of a food processor fitted with a metal blade, process the basil, tomatoes, garlic, salt, pepper, and oregano until the tomatoes are finely chopped. Add the oil and vinegar and process to create a spreadable paste.

2. Cut each chicken breast in half lengthwise and then cut each half crosswise into 1- to 1½-inch pieces. Place the chicken pieces in a large glass or stainless steel bowl and add the paste. Turn to coat the chicken pieces evenly. Cover and refrigerate for 2 to 3 hours.

3. Prepare the grill for direct cooking over high heat (450° to 550°F).

4. Thread the chicken pieces onto skewers, being sure to keep each skewer well within the flesh of the chicken. Discard any remaining paste.

5. Brush the cooking grates clean. Grill the skewers over ***direct high heat***, with the lid closed as much as possible, until the meat is firm to the touch and opaque all the way to the center, 6 to 8 minutes, turning once or twice. Remove from the grill and serve warm.

SERVES: 4

CHICKEN, ONION, AND TOMATO SKEWERS
WITH CREAMY AVOCADO SAUCE

PREP TIME: 30 minutes
GRILLING TIME: 6 to 8 minutes
SPECIAL EQUIPMENT: 6 metal or bamboo skewers (if using bamboo, soak in water for at least 30 minutes)

Rub

- 2 teaspoons kosher salt
- 1 teaspoon dry mustard
- 1 teaspoon ancho chile powder
- ½ teaspoon paprika
- ½ teaspoon ground coriander
- ½ teaspoon ground cumin
- ¼ teaspoon granulated garlic

- 4 boneless, skinless chicken breast halves, about 6 ounces each
  Extra-virgin olive oil
- 12 scallions (white and light green parts only)
- 24 cherry tomatoes, stems removed

Sauce

- 1 ripe Hass avocado, roughly chopped
- 1 two-inch piece English cucumber, peeled and roughly chopped
- ¼ cup sour cream
- ¼ cup roughly chopped shallots
- ¼ cup roughly chopped fresh Italian parsley leaves
- ¼ cup water
  Juice of ½ lime
  Tabasco® sauce
  Kosher salt

1. Prepare the grill for direct cooking over high heat (450° to 550°F).

2. In a small bowl mix the rub ingredients.

3. Cut each chicken breast in half lengthwise and then cut each half crosswise into 1- to 1½-inch pieces. Put the chicken pieces in a large bowl and add just enough oil to coat them lightly. Add the rub and toss to coat evenly.

4. Cut the scallions into pieces 1 to 2 inches long.

5. Thread the chicken, scallions, and tomatoes alternately onto skewers (skewer each scallion crosswise through the middle).

6. In the bowl of a food processor or blender, combine the sauce ingredients. Blend until smooth. Season with Tabasco and salt.

7. Brush the cooking grates clean. Grill the skewers over **direct high heat**, with the lid closed as much as possible, until the meat is firm to the touch and opaque all the way to the center, 6 to 8 minutes, turning once or twice. Remove from the grill and serve with the avocado sauce.

SERVES: 6

CHICKEN AND PEACH KABOBS
WITH BLACKBERRY SAUCE

PREP TIME: 25 minutes
GRILLING TIME: 8 to 10 minutes
SPECIAL EQUIPMENT: metal or bamboo skewers
(if using bamboo, soak in water for at least
30 minutes)

Sauce

- 6 ounces fresh blackberries
- 2 tablespoons granulated sugar
- 1 tablespoon unsalted butter
- 1 tablespoon lemon juice
- 1 teaspoon grated fresh ginger
- 1 teaspoon minced garlic
  Kosher salt
  Ground black pepper

- 3 boneless, skinless chicken breast halves,
  about 6 ounces each
- 2 firm but ripe medium peaches
- 3 tablespoons vegetable oil
- 1 teaspoon kosher salt
- ½ teaspoon ground allspice
- ½ teaspoon ground black pepper

Use the back of a
spoon to extract
and push through a
sieve as much of the
precious blackberry
sauce as you can.

1. In a small saucepan combine the blackberries, sugar, butter, lemon juice, ginger, and garlic. Cook over medium heat until the berries break down, stirring often and smashing the berries with back of a wooden spoon until the juices begin to thicken, 5 to 7 minutes. Strain the sauce through a sieve into a small glass or stainless steel bowl, pressing on the solids in the sieve to extract the liquid. Discard the remaining solids. Season with salt and pepper.

2. Prepare the grill for direct cooking over medium heat (350° to 450°F).

3. Cut each chicken breast in half lengthwise and then cut each half crosswise into 1- to 1½-inch pieces. Cut the peaches into eighths. Combine the chicken and peaches in a large bowl. Add the oil, salt, allspice, and pepper. Mix gently to coat the ingredients evenly. Thread the chicken and peaches alternately onto skewers.

4. Brush the cooking grates clean. Grill the kabobs over ***direct medium heat***, with the lid closed as much as possible, until the meat is firm to the touch and opaque all the way to the center, 8 to 10 minutes, turning two or three times. Remove from the grill and spoon the sauce over the top. Serve warm.

SERVES: 4

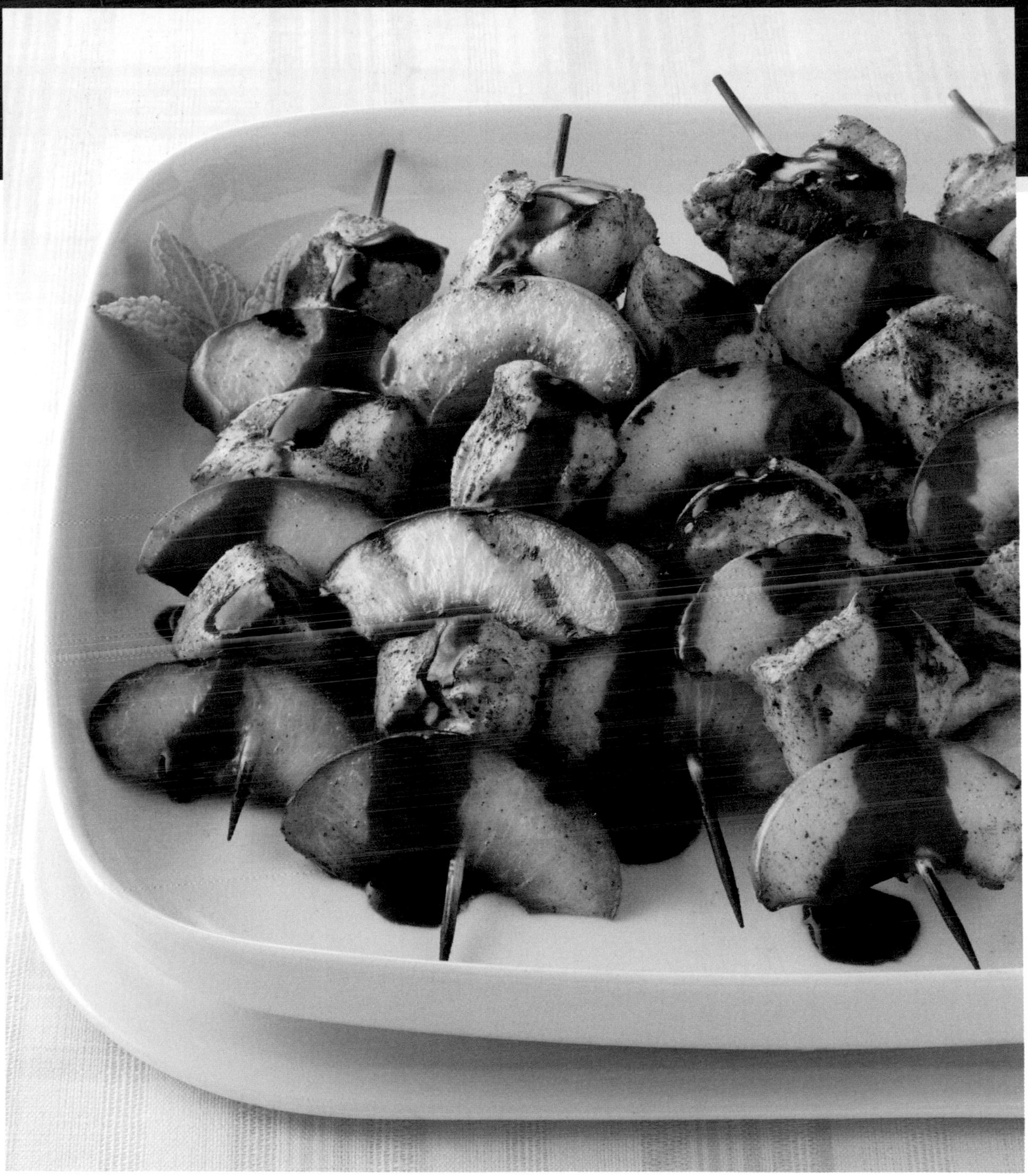

TURKISH CHICKEN KABOBS
WITH RED PEPPER AND WALNUT SAUCE

PREP TIME: 15 minutes
MARINATING TIME: up to 1 hour
GRILLING TIME: 8 to 10 minutes
SPECIAL EQUIPMENT: metal or bamboo skewers
(if using bamboo, soak in water for at least
30 minutes)

1 teaspoon dry mustard
1 teaspoon granulated garlic
1 teaspoon kosher salt
½ teaspoon ground cumin
½ teaspoon ground black pepper
¼ cup extra-virgin olive oil
6 boneless, skinless chicken breast halves,
   about 6 ounces each

Sauce

1½ roasted red bell peppers (from a jar), drained
½ cup toasted walnuts
½ cup extra-virgin olive oil
¼ cup plain bread crumbs
2 tablespoons balsamic vinegar
½ teaspoon ground cumin
¼ teaspoon kosher salt
¼ teaspoon ground black pepper

1. In a large bowl mix the mustard, granulated garlic, salt, cumin, and pepper. Add the oil and stir to combine.

2. Cut each chicken breast in half lengthwise and then cut each half crosswise into 1- to 1½-inch pieces. Place the chicken pieces in the bowl and turn to coat them evenly.

3. Skewer the chicken pieces so that the pieces are touching but not crammed together. Cover and refrigerate for up to 1 hour.

4. In the bowl of a food processor or blender, combine the sauce ingredients and process to create a pesto-like consistency. For a thinner sauce, add a bit of warm water.

5. Prepare the grill for direct cooking over medium heat (350° to 450°F).

6. Brush the cooking grates clean. Grill the kabobs over *direct medium heat*, with the lid closed as much as possible, until the meat is firm to the touch and opaque all the way to the center, 8 to 10 minutes, turning once or twice. Remove from the grill and serve warm with the sauce.

SERVES: 6

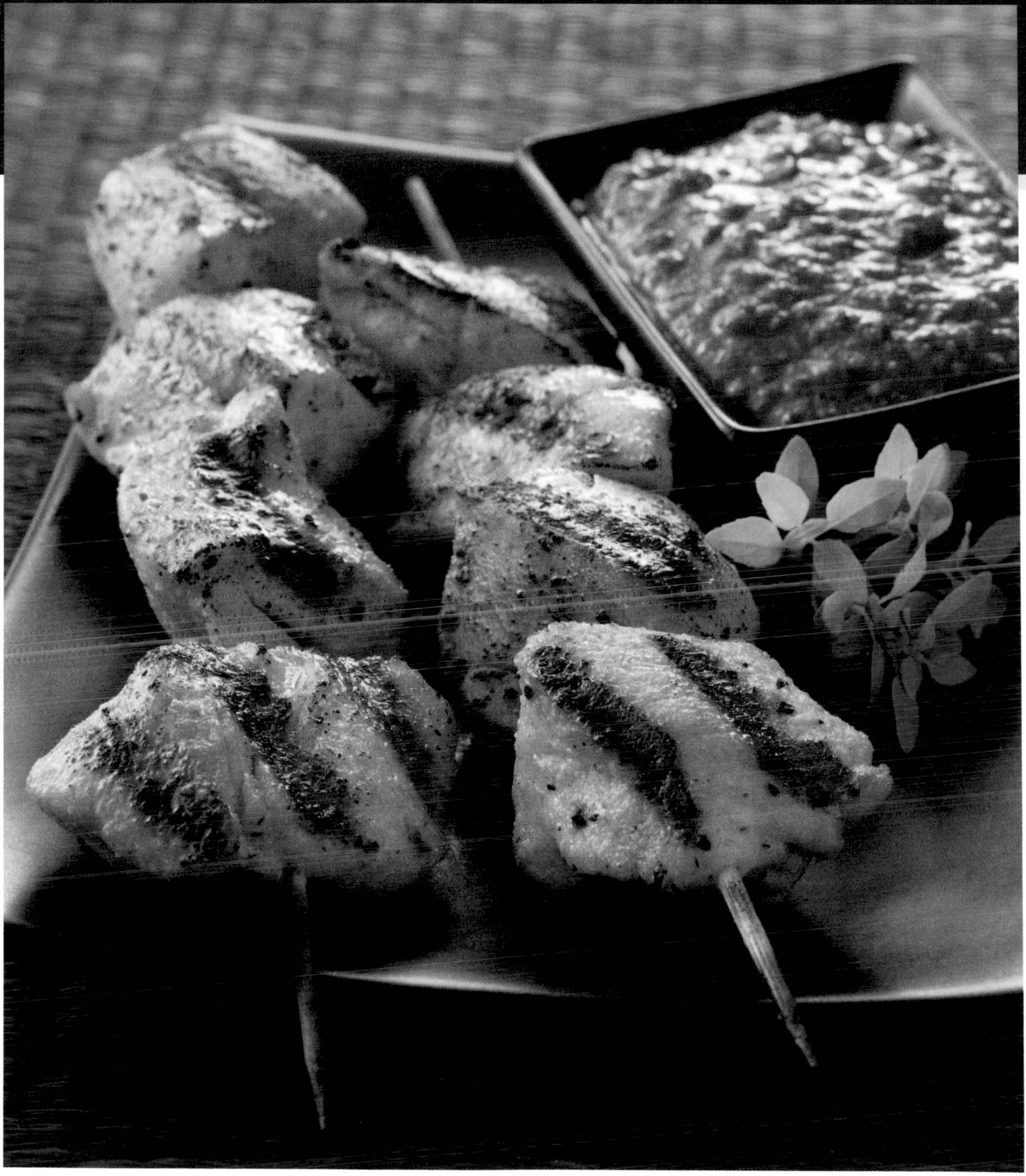

MARINATED CHICKEN SPIEDINI
WITH ROSEMARY AND GARLIC

PREP TIME: 20 minutes
MARINATING TIME: 30 minutes to 1 hour
GRILLING TIME: 8 to 10 minutes
SPECIAL EQUIPMENT: metal or bamboo skewers
(if using bamboo, soak in water for at least
30 minutes)

Marinade

- ½ cup extra-virgin olive oil
- 2 tablespoons white wine vinegar
- 1 tablespoon finely chopped fresh rosemary leaves
- 1 tablespoon minced garlic
- 1 teaspoon kosher salt
- ½ teaspoon ground black pepper

- 4 boneless, skinless chicken breast halves,
  about 6 ounces each
- 1 medium red onion
- 1 pint grape tomatoes

1. In a small bowl whisk the marinade ingredients.

2. Cut each chicken breast in half lengthwise and then cut each half crosswise into 1- to 1½-inch pieces. Cut the onion into quarters through the stem end. Cut each quarter in half crosswise. Place the chicken pieces, onion pieces, and tomatoes in a large, resealable plastic bag and pour in the marinade. Press the air out of the bag and seal tightly. Turn the bag to distribute the marinade, and refrigerate for 30 minutes to 1 hour, turning occasionally.

3. Prepare the grill for direct cooking over medium heat (350° to 450°F).

4. Remove the chicken and vegetables from the bag and discard the marinade. Thread the chicken pieces, onion pieces, and tomatoes alternately onto skewers.

5. Brush the cooking grates clean. Grill the skewers over *direct medium heat*, with the lid closed as much as possible, until the meat is firm to the touch and opaque all the way to the center and the onion is tender, 8 to 10 minutes, turning once or twice. Remove from the grill and serve warm.

SERVES: 4 to 6

CHICKEN TENDER SKEWERS
MARINATED IN GREEN TEA AND GINGER

PREP TIME: 20 minutes
MARINATING TIME: 1 to 2 hours
GRILLING TIME: 4 to 6 minutes
SPECIAL EQUIPMENT: metal or bamboo skewers
(if using bamboo, soak in water for at least
30 minutes)

Marinade

- 1 cup water
- 2 green tea bags (single serve)
- 3 slices fresh ginger, each about ¼ inch thick
- ⅓ cup soy sauce
- ¼ cup rice wine (mirin)
- 2 tablespoons rice vinegar
- 2 tablespoons canola oil
- 2 teaspoons minced garlic

1½ pounds chicken tenders
    Canola oil
- ¼ cup thinly sliced scallions
- ¼ cup pickled ginger (optional)

1. In a small saucepan bring the water to a boil. Remove the saucepan from the heat and add the tea bags and ginger slices. Let steep for 10 minutes. Discard the tea bags. Let the tea cool completely and then whisk in the remaining marinade ingredients.

2. Place the chicken in a large, resealable plastic bag and pour in the marinade. Press the air out of the bag and seal tightly. Turn the bag to distribute the marinade, place in a bowl, and refrigerate for 1 to 2 hours, turning occasionally.

3. Prepare the grill for direct cooking over high heat (450° to 550°F).

4. Remove the chicken from the bag and discard the marinade. Thread the chicken onto skewers, and lightly brush all sides with oil.

5. Brush the cooking grates clean. Grill the chicken over *direct high heat*, with the lid closed as much as possible, until the meat is firm to the touch and the juices run clear, 4 to 6 minutes, turning once or twice. Remove from the grill and arrange on a large platter. Sprinkle with the sliced scallions. Serve warm with pickled ginger on the side, if desired.

SERVES: 4

CHICKEN GYROS
WITH TOMATO TZATZIKI

PREP TIME: 30 minutes
MARINATING TIME: 30 minutes
GRILLING TIME: 8 to 10 minutes

Sauce

- 1 cup Greek yogurt
- 2 tablespoons finely chopped fresh mint leaves
- 1 tablespoon extra-virgin olive oil
- 1½ teaspoons fresh lemon juice
- ½ teaspoon kosher salt
- ¼ teaspoon ground black pepper
- 1 cup finely chopped ripe tomato
- ½ cup finely diced cucumber

Marinade

- 3 tablespoons extra-virgin olive oil
- 3 tablespoons fresh lemon juice
- 1 tablespoon dried oregano
- 1 garlic clove, minced
- ½ teaspoon kosher salt
- ¼ teaspoon ground black pepper
- ⅛ teaspoon crushed red pepper flakes

1½ pounds chicken tenders

- 1 small red onion, cut crosswise into ½-inch slices
  Extra-virgin olive oil

- 6 flat breads or pitas

1. In a medium glass or stainless steel bowl, whisk the yogurt, mint, oil, lemon juice, salt, and pepper. Add the tomato and cucumber and stir to combine.

2. In a large glass or stainless steel bowl, whisk the marinade ingredients. Add the chicken to the bowl and turn to coat evenly. Marinate at room temperature for 30 minutes.

3. Prepare the grill for direct cooking over medium heat (350° to 450°F).

4. Lightly brush the onion slices on both sides with oil. Remove the chicken from the bowl, letting the herbs cling to the chicken. Discard the marinade. Brush the cooking grates clean. Grill the chicken and onion slices over *direct medium heat*, with the lid closed as much as possible, until the meat is firm to the touch and the juices run clear and the onion is tender, 6 to 8 minutes, turning once. Remove from the grill.

5. Warm the flat breads on the grill over *direct medium heat* until lightly charred, about 2 minutes, turning once or twice.

6. Layer some chicken, sauce, and onion inside the flat breads and serve warm or at room temperature. Serving suggestion: Grecian Orzo Salad (for recipe, see page 125).

SERVES: 6

PARMESAN-BREADED CHICKEN
WITH LEMON AIOLI

PREP TIME: 20 minutes
CHILLING TIME: 30 minutes
GRILLING TIME: 6 to 8 minutes

Aioli
- ¾ cup mayonnaise
- 1 teaspoon finely grated lemon zest
- 2 tablespoons fresh lemon juice
- 1 tablespoon minced garlic
- 1 teaspoon Dijon mustard

Breading
- 1 cup plain bread crumbs
- ½ cup freshly grated Parmigiano-Reggiano® cheese
- ¼ cup finely chopped fresh Italian parsley leaves
- 1 teaspoon kosher salt
- ½ teaspoon ground black pepper

- 1½ pounds chicken tenders
- Extra-virgin olive oil

1. In a small glass or stainless steel bowl, whisk the aioli ingredients. Cover with plastic wrap and refrigerate until ready to use.

2. In a large bowl mix the breading ingredients.

3. Place the chicken in a medium bowl, add 2 tablespoons of oil, and mix to coat evenly. Dredge each chicken tender in the breading, turning to cover each one evenly. Gently press the breading into the meat. Place the breaded chicken in a single layer on a sheet pan. Cover with plastic wrap and refrigerate for 30 minutes to set the breading.

4. Prepare the grill for direct cooking over medium heat (350° to 450°F).

5. Brush the cooking grates clean. Lightly brush the breaded chicken on both sides with oil. Grill the chicken, 1 to 2 inches apart, over *direct medium heat*, with the lid closed as much as possible, until the juices run clear and the breading is golden brown, 6 to 8 minutes, turning once. Remove from the grill and serve warm with the aioli for dipping.

SERVES: 4 (as an appetizer)

CHICKEN TENDER SALAD
WITH MELON AND MINT

PREP TIME: 20 minutes
GRILLING TIME: 4 to 6 minutes

1 pound chicken tenders
  Extra-virgin olive oil
½ teaspoon kosher salt
¼ teaspoon prepared chili powder
¼ teaspoon ground black pepper
⅓ medium cantaloupe, cut into ¾-inch pieces
8 ounces fresh mozzarella cheese,
  cut into ½-inch dice
3 ounces thinly sliced prosciutto,
  cut into ¾-inch pieces
¼ cup finely chopped fresh mint leaves
2 teaspoons fresh lime juice

1. Prepare the grill for direct cooking over high heat (450° to 550°F).

2. Lightly brush the chicken tenders on both sides with oil and season them evenly with the salt, chili powder, and pepper.

3. Brush the cooking grates clean. Grill the chicken over **direct high heat**, with the lid closed as much as possible, until the meat is firm to the touch and the juices run clear, 4 to 6 minutes, turning once or twice. Remove from the grill and let cool to room temperature.

4. In a large serving bowl mix the cantaloupe, cheese, prosciutto, and mint.

5. Cut the chicken tenders into bite-sized pieces and add them to the bowl. Mix well. Add the lime juice and mix again. Serve at room temperature.

SERVES: 4

BASIC GRILLED ASPARAGUS

PREP TIME: 5 minutes
GRILLING TIME: 6 to 8 minutes

1 pound asparagus
2 tablespoons extra-virgin olive oil
½ teaspoon kosher salt

1. Prepare the grill for direct cooking over medium heat (350° to 450°F).

2. Remove and discard the tough bottom of each asparagus spear by grasping each end and bending it gently until it snaps at its natural point of tenderness, usually two-thirds of the way down the spear. Using a vegetable peeler, peel off the outer skin from the bottom half of each remaining spear.

3. Spread the asparagus on a large plate. Drizzle the oil and salt over the top. Turn the spears until they are evenly coated.

4. Brush the cooking grates clean. Grill the asparagus (perpendicular to the grate) over **direct medium heat**, with the lid closed as much as possible, until browned in spots but not charred, 6 to 8 minutes, turning occasionally. Serve warm or at room temperature.

SERVES: 4

ASPARAGUS WITH
SHERRY-BACON VINAIGRETTE

PREP TIME: 15 minutes
GRILLING TIME: 6 to 8 minutes

4–6 slices bacon
 1 teaspoon finely chopped fresh thyme leaves
 ½ teaspoon minced garlic
 1 tablespoon sherry vinegar
 ¼ teaspoon kosher salt
 ¼ teaspoon ground black pepper
 1 pound asparagus
 ½ small red onion, thinly sliced crosswise

NOTE!

Look for firm asparagus stalks with deep green or purplish tips. Also check the bottom of the spears. If they are dried up, chances are they have been sitting around for too long. Thicker spears fare better on the grill.

1. Prepare the grill for direct cooking over medium heat (350° to 450°F).

2. In a medium skillet over medium heat, lay the bacon in a single layer and cook until crispy, 8 to 10 minutes, turning occasionally. Drain the bacon on paper towels, reserving the bacon fat in the skillet.

3. Pour off all but 3 tablespoons of the bacon fat and return the skillet over medium heat. Add the thyme and garlic to the skillet and let them sizzle for about 10 seconds. Add the vinegar, salt, and pepper, and then remove the skillet from the heat.

4. Remove and discard the tough bottom of each asparagus spear by grasping each end and bending it gently until it snaps at its natural point of tenderness, usually two-thirds of the way down the spear. Using a vegetable peeler, peel off the outer skin from the bottom half of each remaining spear. Put the asparagus on a plate or platter. Pour the vinaigrette over the asparagus. Turn the asparagus to coat evenly. Finely chop the drained bacon.

5. Brush the cooking grates clean. Grill the asparagus over *direct medium heat*, with the lid closed as much as possible, until browned in spots but not charred, 6 to 8 minutes, turning occasionally. Arrange the asparagus on a serving platter. Sprinkle the bacon over the asparagus. Arrange the onion slices on top. Serve warm or at room temperature.

SERVES: 4

Sides

EGGPLANT WITH SPICY ASIAN DRESSING

PREP TIME: 10 minutes
GRILLING TIME: 8 to 10 minutes

Dressing

1–2 serrano chile peppers, stems and seeds removed, minced
3 tablespoons soy sauce
2 tablespoons fresh lemon juice
2 tablespoons minced yellow onion
1 tablespoon water

2 globe eggplants, each about 12 ounces
Vegetable oil
1 teaspoon granulated garlic

1. Prepare the grill for direct cooking over medium heat (350° to 450°F).

2. In a small glass or stainless steel bowl, combine the dressing ingredients.

3. Cut the eggplants crosswise into ½-inch slices. Generously brush both sides of the slices with oil and season evenly with the granulated garlic.

4. Brush the cooking grates clean. Grill the eggplant slices over **direct medium heat**, with the lid closed as much as possible, until well marked and tender, 8 to 10 minutes, turning once. Place the slices on a platter and spoon the dressing over the top. Serve warm.

SERVES: 4

ACORN SQUASH WITH BROWN BUTTER AND GARLIC

PREP TIME: 10 minutes
GRILLING TIME: 40 minutes to 1 hour

Glaze

3 tablespoons unsalted butter, cut into 3 pieces
2 tablespoons dark brown sugar
2 teaspoons minced garlic
1 teaspoon kosher salt
¼ teaspoon ground black pepper
¼ teaspoon grated nutmeg
1 tablespoon cider vinegar

2 small acorn squashes, each about 1½ pounds

1. In a small saucepan or skillet, combine the glaze ingredients except the vinegar. Cook over medium-high heat for 2 to 3 minutes, stirring occasionally. Remove from the heat; cool to room temperature.

2. Prepare the grill for indirect cooking over high heat (450° to 550°F).

3. Using a large knife, carefully cut the squashes in half lengthwise. Scoop out and discard the seeds and strings. Add the vinegar to the cooled glaze. Brush the glaze over the exposed flesh of the squashes.

4. Brush the cooking grates clean. Grill the squashes, with the exposed flesh facing up, over **indirect high heat**, with the lid closed as much as possible, until a sharp knife inserted all the way into the flesh slides out easily, 40 minutes to 1 hour, basting occasionally with the glaze that pools in the bowl of the squashes. Remove from the grill and serve warm.

SERVES: 4

ARTICHOKES WITH OREGANO AND SALT

PREP TIME: 30 minutes
GRILLING TIME: 4 to 6 minutes

  4 large artichokes, 10 to 12 ounces each
     Juice of 1 lemon
  1 tablespoon extra-virgin olive oil
  ½ teaspoon dried oregano
  ¼ teaspoon granulated garlic
  ¼ teaspoon kosher salt
  ½ cup (1 stick) unsalted butter, melted

1. Bring a large pot of salted water to a boil.

2. Cut the stem off of each artichoke, leaving about ½ inch attached. Peel off the dark outer leaves until you expose the light green, yellowish leaves underneath. Lay each artichoke on its side and cut off the top half so you have just the firm base to work with. Cut each base in half lengthwise through the stem and drop each half into a large glass or stainless steel bowl of water mixed with the lemon juice (to prevent discoloration).

3. One at a time, lift the artichokes from the water and use a teaspoon to scoop out all of the fuzzy choke and purplish leaves. Cook the artichokes in the boiling, salted water until you can pierce them easily with a knife, 10 to 12 minutes, but don't overcook them or they will fall apart on the grill. Drain the artichokes in a colander and place in a large bowl. While still warm, add the oil, oregano, granulated garlic, and salt. Toss gently to coat the artichokes. (The artichokes may be made up to this point and refrigerated for up to 4 hours. Bring to room temperature before grilling.)

4. Prepare the grill for direct cooking over medium heat (350° to 450°F).

5. Brush the cooking grates clean. Grill the artichokes over **_direct medium heat_**, with the lid closed as much as possible, until well browned and warm, 4 to 6 minutes, turning once. Serve warm with the melted butter.

SERVES: 4

Sides

MELTED ONIONS

PREP TIME: 10 minutes
GRILLING TIME: $1\frac{1}{4}$ to $1\frac{3}{4}$ hours, for charcoal grills only
SPECIAL EQUIPMENT: large disposable foil pan

- 6 medium yellow onions (skin on), 8 to 10 ounces each, about the size of a tennis ball
- ¼ cup (½ stick) unsalted butter
- ½ teaspoon kosher salt
- ¼ teaspoon ground black pepper
- 1 teaspoon sherry vinegar
- 1 tablespoon minced fresh Italian parsley leaves

1. Fill a chimney starter to the rim with charcoal and burn the charcoal until it is lightly covered with ash. Spread the charcoal in a tightly packed, single layer across one-half of the charcoal grate. Let the coals burn down to medium heat (350° to 450°F). Leave all the vents open.

2. With the onions still in their skins, place them on the charcoal grate against the charcoal. Close the lid and cook the onions until very tender, 1 to 1½ hours. Occasionally swap the positions of the onions for even cooking and turn the blackened skins away from the charcoal. When very tender, the onions will be blackened in spots all over and a knife blade will slide in and out of each onion like it is a ripe peach. Some onions may take longer than others.

3. At this point, to finish cooking the onions, you will need to add more charcoal to the fire for medium heat.

4. Remove the onions from the grill and let cool completely. Carefully remove the skin from each onion, being careful to leave the root ends intact so they hold the layers of the onions together. Cut each onion lengthwise through the stem and root end.

5. When the fire is ready, put the cooking grate in place. Melt the butter in a large disposable foil pan over ***direct medium heat***. Carefully add the onions in a single layer and season with the salt and pepper. Using tongs, turn the onions in the butter to coat them.

6. Slide the pan over ***indirect medium heat*** and cook, with the lid closed as much as possible, until the onions are very tender and just beginning to brown, 10 to 15 minutes, carefully turning the onions once or twice. If desired, to keep the onions warm, cover the pan with foil and let the onions continue to cook over indirect heat for as long as 30 minutes. Wearing barbecue mitts, remove the pan from the grill. Splash the vinegar and sprinkle the parsley over the onions. Serve warm.

SERVES: 4 to 6

GRILLED CARROTS

PREP TIME: 10 minutes
GRILLING TIME: 3 to 5 minutes

- 8 medium carrots, each 6 to 8 inches long and about 1 inch wide at the thick end
- ¼ cup (½ stick) unsalted butter
- ½ teaspoon red wine vinegar
- ¼ teaspoon ground nutmeg
- ½ teaspoon kosher salt, divided
- ¼ teaspoon ground black pepper, divided
- 1 teaspoon minced fresh Italian parsley leaves (optional)

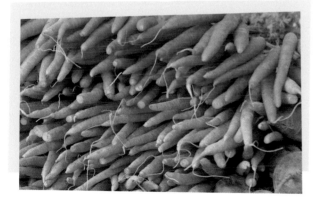

1. Peel the carrots and cook them in boiling water until they are partially cooked but still crisp, 4 to 6 minutes. Drain the carrots and rinse them under cold water for at least 10 seconds to stop the cooking.

2. Prepare the grill for direct cooking over high heat (450° to 550°F).

3. Lay the carrots flat on a work surface. In a small saucepan over medium heat, melt the butter with the vinegar and nutmeg. Brush the carrots with about half the butter mixture and season them with about half the salt and pepper.

4. Brush the cooking grates clean. Grill the carrots over ***direct high heat***, with the lid open, until lightly charred with spots and stripes, 3 to 5 minutes, turning occasionally. Move the carrots to a platter, brush them with the remaining butter mixture, and season them with the remaining salt and pepper. Sprinkle the parsley over the top, if using. Serve warm.

SERVES: 4

Sides

GLAZED SWEET POTATOES

PREP TIME: 10 minutes
GRILLING TIME: 15 to 20 minutes

Glaze

 Grated zest of 2 limes
¼ cup fresh lime juice
¼ cup canola oil
 2 tablespoons honey
½ teaspoon kosher salt
¼ teaspoon ground black pepper

 2 sweet potatoes, about 2 pounds total

1. Prepare the grill for direct cooking over medium heat (350° to 450°F).

2. In a small glass or stainless steel bowl, whisk the glaze ingredients. Peel the sweet potatoes, trim the ends, and cut each potato into ½-inch slices. Brush the potatoes on both sides with the glaze.

3. Brush the cooking grates clean. Grill the potatoes over *direct medium heat*, with the lid closed as much as possible, until they are easily pierced with a knife, 15 to 20 minutes, turning and brushing them with the glaze about every 5 minutes. Remove from the grill and serve warm.

SERVES: 4 to 6

MASHED SWEET POTATOES WITH GRILLED ONIONS

PREP TIME: 10 minutes
GRILLING TIME: about 1¼ hours

 4 sweet potatoes, about 4 pounds total, scrubbed
 1 large yellow onion, cut crosswise into ½-inch slices
 Extra-virgin olive oil
 Kosher salt
 Ground black pepper
¼ cup (½ stick) unsalted butter, softened

1. Prepare the grill for direct and indirect cooking over medium heat (350° to 450°F).

2. Grill the sweet potatoes over *indirect medium heat*, with the lid closed as much as possible, until tender when pierced with a fork, about 1 hour, turning three or four times. Remove from the grill and allow to cool slightly. When cool enough to handle, cut the potatoes in half lengthwise. Remove and discard the skins. Place the potatoes in a medium bowl and cover with aluminum foil.

3. Brush or spray the onion slices with oil and season with salt and pepper. Grill over *direct medium heat*, with the lid closed as much as possible, for 10 to 12 minutes, turning once. Remove from the grill and allow to cool, and then cut into ¼-inch dice.

4. Using a heavy-duty mixer or potato masher, mash the potatoes with the butter until smooth. Add the diced onion and mix well. Serve warm.

SERVES: 8 to 10

TWICE-GRILLED POTATOES

PREP TIME: 15 minutes
GRILLING TIME: 40 to 45 minutes

4 russet potatoes, about 10 ounces each,
  scrubbed and halved lengthwise
  Vegetable oil

Stuffing

¾ cup sour cream
½ cup minced cooked ham
1½ cups grated Gruyère cheese, divided
2 teaspoons Dijon mustard
  Kosher salt
  Ground black pepper

1. Prepare the grill for direct cooking over medium heat (350° to 450°F).

2. Lightly coat the potato halves with oil. Brush the cooking grates clean. Grill the potatoes over **direct medium heat**, with the lid closed as much as possible, until tender when pierced with a fork, 30 to 35 minutes, turning three or four times. Allow to cool slightly.

3. When cool enough to handle, use a small sharp knife to cut around the cut side of the potato to within ¼ inch of the skin. Using a teaspoon or melon baller, scoop out the interior of the potato leaving a shell about ¼ inch thick. Place the potato pulp in a large bowl. Set the potato shells aside while preparing the stuffing.

4. Using a potato masher or pastry blender, mash the potato pulp in the bowl. Add the sour cream and mix well. Stir in the ham and half of the cheese. Add the mustard, and season with salt and pepper. Taste and adjust the seasoning, adding more mustard, if desired. Divide the stuffing evenly among the skins, so that the stuffing mounds slightly. Sprinkle the remaining cheese over the stuffing.

5. Grill the stuffed potatoes over **direct medium heat**, with the lid closed, until the cheese is melted and the potatoes are heated through, about 10 minutes. Serve immediately.

SERVES: 8

Sides

GRILL-ROASTED NEW POTATOES

PREP TIME: 10 minutes
GRILLING TIME: 15 to 20 minutes

  2 tablespoons extra-virgin olive oil
  ½ teaspoon kosher salt
  ½ teaspoon ground black pepper
  2 pounds new potatoes, each 1½ to 2 inches
     in diameter, scrubbed and quartered
  2 teaspoons minced fresh Italian parsley leaves

1. Prepare the grill for direct cooking over medium heat (350° to 450°F).

2. In a medium bowl combine the oil, salt, and pepper. Add the potatoes and stir to coat them evenly. Brush the cooking grates clean. Grill the potatoes over **direct medium heat**, with the lid closed as much as possible, until tender and browned on all sides, 15 to 20 minutes, scooping and turning with a wide spatula every 5 minutes or so.

3. Place the potatoes in a medium serving bowl and sprinkle with the parsley. Serve warm.

SERVES: 6 to 8

RED CHILE RICE

PREP TIME: 5 minutes
COOKING TIME: about 30 minutes

  2 tablespoons extra-virgin olive oil
  1 cup finely chopped white onion
  1 teaspoon ancho chile powder
  2 cups medium-grain rice
  3 cups cold water
  ¾ teaspoon kosher salt
  ½ teaspoon dried oregano
  ½ teaspoon ground cumin
  ¼ teaspoon ground black pepper

1. In a medium saucepan over medium heat, warm the oil. Add the onion and cook for 2 to 3 minutes, stirring occasionally to avoid browning. Add the chile powder. Cook for about 1 minute, stirring occasionally. Add the rice. Stir to coat the grains of rice evenly with oil. Add the remaining ingredients and stir to combine. Bring the mixture to a simmer. Reduce the heat to low, cover the saucepan with a tight-fitting lid, and cook until the rice is tender and has absorbed all the water, 18 to 20 minutes. Remove the saucepan from the heat and leave it alone for 5 minutes. Remove the lid and fluff the rice with a fork. Serve warm.

SERVES: 6 to 8

SMOKY SWEET BAKED BEANS

PREP TIME: 15 minutes
GRILLING TIME: 25 to 28 minutes
SPECIAL EQUIPMENT: large ovenproof saucepan

- 4 ounces bacon, cut into ½-inch pieces
- ½ cup finely chopped yellow onion
- 2 teaspoons minced garlic
- ¼ teaspoon crushed red pepper flakes
- 1 can (28 ounces) baked beans
- ¼ cup ketchup
- 2 teaspoons Worcestershire sauce
- ½ teaspoon prepared chili powder
  Kosher salt
  Ground black pepper

1. Prepare the grill for direct cooking over medium heat (350° to 450°F).

2. In a large ovenproof saucepan cook the bacon over *direct medium heat*, with the lid closed as much as possible, until crispy, 8 to 10 minutes, stirring occasionally. Add the onion and cook until tender, 2 to 3 minutes, stirring occasionally. Add the garlic and red pepper flakes, and cook for about 30 seconds, stirring occasionally. Add the baked beans (with their liquid), ketchup, Worcestershire sauce, and chili powder. Bring the mixture to a simmer, stirring occasionally.

3. Lower the temperature of the grill to low heat (250° to 350°F), and continue to cook the beans over *direct low heat*, with the lid closed as much as possible, for 15 minutes, stirring all the way to the bottom of the pot occasionally. Taste and adjust the seasoning with salt and pepper, if necessary. Serve warm.

SERVES: 4 to 6

STEWED WHITE BEANS

PREP TIME: 10 minutes
GRILLING TIME: 6 to 8 minutes

- 4 ripe plum tomatoes, about 1 pound, cored
- 2 tablespoons extra-virgin olive oil
- ½ cup finely diced yellow onion
- 1 tablespoon minced garlic
- ¼ teaspoon red pepper flakes
- 2 cans (15 ounces each) cannellini beans, rinsed
  Kosher salt
  Ground black pepper
- ¼ cup loosely packed torn fresh basil leaves

1. Prepare the grill for direct cooking over medium heat (350° to 450°F).

2. Brush the cooking grates clean. Grill the tomatoes over *direct medium heat*, with the lid closed as much as possible, until the skins are loosened, 6 to 8 minutes, turning occasionally. Remove from the grill and cut into 1-inch chunks.

3. In a medium saucepan over medium heat, warm the oil. Add the onion, garlic, and pepper flakes and cook until softened, about 3 minutes, stirring occasionally. Add the tomatoes and beans, stir to combine, and season with salt and pepper. When the beans come to a boil, reduce the heat and simmer for 15 minutes. Remove from the heat and add the basil. Serve warm.

SERVES: 4 to 6

Sides

CORN ON THE COB WITH BASIL-PARMESAN BUTTER

PREP TIME: 10 minutes
GRILLING TIME: 10 to 15 minutes

Butter

- ¼ cup (½ stick) unsalted butter, softened
- ¼ cup freshly grated Parmigiano-Reggiano® cheese
- 2 tablespoons finely chopped fresh basil leaves
- ½ teaspoon kosher salt
- ¼ teaspoon ground black pepper
- ¼ teaspoon granulated garlic

- 4 ears fresh corn, husked

1. Prepare the grill for direct cooking over medium heat (350° to 450°F).

2. In a small bowl mash the butter ingredients with the back of a fork, and then stir to distribute the seasonings throughout the butter.

3. Brush about 1 tablespoon of the seasoned butter all over each ear of corn. Brush the cooking grates clean. Grill the corn over *direct medium heat*, with the lid closed as much as possible, until browned in spots and tender, 10 to 15 minutes, turning occasionally. Serve warm with the remaining butter spread on the corn.

SERVES: 4

CAJUN CORN WITH LOUISIANA BUTTER

PREP TIME: 15 minutes
GRILLING TIME: 25 to 30 minutes

Butter

- 1 teaspoon paprika
- ½ teaspoon onion powder
- ½ teaspoon kosher salt
- ½ teaspoon dried thyme
- ¼ teaspoon dried oregano
- ⅛ teaspoon ground cayenne pepper
- ¼ cup (½ stick) unsalted butter, softened

- 4 ears fresh corn, in their husks

1. Prepare the grill for direct cooking over medium heat (350° to 450°F).

2. In a small bowl combine the butter ingredients, stirring to distribute the seasonings evenly.

3. Pull back the husks on each ear of corn, leaving the husks attached at the stem. Remove and discard the corn silk. Evenly spread about 1 tablespoon of the seasoned butter over the kernels of each ear. Fold the husks back around the kernels. Using string or a thin strip of corn husk, tie the husks at the top.

4. Brush the cooking grates clean. Grill the corn over *direct medium heat*, with the lid closed as much as possible, until the kernels are tender, 25 to 30 minutes, turning three or four times. Don't worry if the husks brown or burn. Carefully pull the husks back. Remove the husks with a knife. Serve warm.

SERVES: 4

CORN AND TOMATO SUMMER SALAD

PREP TIME: 10 minutes

- 1 tablespoon minced shallot
- 2 teaspoons sherry vinegar
- ½ teaspoon Dijon mustard
- ½ teaspoon kosher salt
- ¼ teaspoon ground black pepper
- 2 tablespoons extra-virgin olive oil
- 2 ears fresh corn, husked
- ½ cup cherry tomatoes, cut into quarters
- ¼ cup finely chopped fresh basil leaves

1. In a medium glass or stainless steel bowl, whisk the shallot, vinegar, mustard, salt, and pepper. Slowly whisk in the oil to create a smooth vinaigrette.

2. Place the corn in a large pot of boiling salted water. Turn off the heat, cover the pot, and allow to cook until barely tender, 4 to 5 minutes. Remove from the water and allow to cool. Cut the kernels off the cobs and add to the vinaigrette. Add the tomatoes and basil. Stir to combine. Serve at room temperature.

SERVES: 4

ROASTED CORN AND BLACK BEAN SALAD

PREP TIME: 15 minutes
GRILLING TIME: 10 to 15 minutes

- 3 ears fresh corn, husked
  Extra-virgin olive oil
  Kosher salt
- 2 cans (15 ounces each) black beans, rinsed
- 1½ cups roughly chopped ripe tomatoes
- ½ cup finely chopped celery
- 2 tablespoons finely chopped fresh cilantro leaves

Dressing

- 3 tablespoons extra-virgin olive oil
  Finely grated zest and juice of 1 lime
- 1 teaspoon minced garlic
- ½ teaspoon ground cumin
- ½ teaspoon kosher salt
- ¼ teaspoon ground black pepper

1. Prepare the grill for direct cooking over medium heat (350° to 450°F).

2. Lightly brush the corn all over with oil and season with salt. Brush the cooking grates clean. Grill the corn over **direct medium heat**, with the lid closed as much as possible, until browned in spots and tender, 10 to 15 minutes, turning occasionally.

3. In a large glass bowl cut the kernels off the cobs. Add the beans, tomatoes, celery, and cilantro.

4. In a small bowl whisk the dressing ingredients. Pour the dressing over the salad and mix to coat evenly. Serve at room temperature.

SERVES: 6 to 8

Sides

PICKLED CUCUMBERS

PREP TIME: 10 minutes
PICKLING TIME: 2 hours

¼ cup rice vinegar
1 tablespoon fresh lemon juice
1 tablespoon granulated sugar
1 teaspoon kosher salt
¼ cup water
2 thin Japanese cucumbers, 4 to 6 ounces each

1. In a medium glass or stainless steel bowl, mix the vinegar, lemon juice, sugar, and salt until the sugar and salt are dissolved. Add the water.

2. Cut the cucumbers into thin strips, each about ¼ inch wide and 3 inches long (could be any shape, really). Add the cucumbers to the pickling liquid and set aside at room temperature for 2 hours, stirring the cucumbers a few times. Drain the pickles before serving and arrange them in a medium serving bowl.

SERVES: 4 to 6

RED CABBAGE COLESLAW WITH CREAMY CAESAR DRESSING

PREP TIME: 15 minutes

Dressing
1 medium garlic clove
½ teaspoon kosher salt
½ cup good-quality mayonnaise
¼ cup freshly grated Parmigiano-Reggiano® cheese
2 tablespoons fresh lemon juice
1 tablespoon Dijon mustard
½ teaspoon Worcestershire sauce
½ teaspoon Tabasco® sauce
¼ teaspoon ground black pepper

3 cups coarsely grated red cabbage
1 cup coarsely grated carrots
½ cup finely chopped scallions (white and light green parts only)

1. Roughly chop the garlic, and then sprinkle the salt on top. Using both the sharp edge and the flat side of the knife blade, crush the garlic and salt together to create a paste. Transfer the paste to a small bowl and add the remaining dressing ingredients. Mix well.

2. In a medium glass or stainless steel bowl, combine the cabbage, carrot, and scallions. Mix well. Add the dressing. Mix again. Cover the bowl with plastic wrap and refrigerate for 2 hours or until ready to serve.

SERVES: 4 to 6

COUSCOUS SALAD

PREP TIME: 30 minutes

1½ cups quick-cooking couscous
⅓ cup raisins
2 cups chicken broth
¼ cup thinly sliced scallions (white part only)
3 tablespoons finely chopped fresh Italian parsley leaves
2 tablespoons finely chopped fresh mint leaves
2 tablespoons extra-virgin olive oil
2 tablespoons fresh lemon juice
½ teaspoon kosher salt
¼ teaspoon ground black pepper

1. In a large saucepan combine the couscous and raisins. Heat the broth to boiling and pour it over the couscous. Toss lightly to mix, cover, and allow to stand for 20 minutes.

2. In a small bowl mix the rest of the ingredients together. Add the mixture to the couscous. Fluff and toss gently with a fork to combine. Serve warm.

SERVES: 4

GRECIAN ORZO SALAD

PREP TIME: 30 minutes

Vinaigrette

½ teaspoon finely grated lemon zest
2 tablespoons fresh lemon juice
¼ cup extra-virgin olive oil
1½ teaspoons finely chopped fresh dill
½ teaspoon minced garlic
¼ teaspoon kosher salt
⅛ teaspoon ground black pepper

1 cup orzo pasta
2 ounces feta cheese, crumbled
¾ cup finely diced red bell pepper
⅓ cup kalamata olives, pitted and quartered
2 tablespoons thinly sliced scallions (white and light green parts only)
1½ tablespoons finely chopped fresh oregano leaves

1. In a small glass or stainless steel bowl, whisk the vinaigrette ingredients.

2. Bring a medium saucepan of salted water to a boil. Add the pasta and cook until *al dente*, following package instructions. Drain and place in a bowl. Add the vinaigrette and the feta cheese and toss well. Add the bell pepper, olives, scallions, and oregano. Toss again. Serve right away.

SERVES: 4

Rubs

A rub is a mixture of spices, herbs, and other seasonings (often including sugar) that can quickly give a boost of flavors to foods before grilling. The next couple of pages provide some mighty good examples of rubs that work particularly well with chicken. Try one when time is tight.

HOW LONG SHOULD I LEAVE A RUB ON MY CHICKEN?

If you leave a rub on for a long time, the seasonings intermix with the juices in the meat and produce more pronounced flavors, as well as a crust. This is good to a point, but a rub with a lot of salt and sugar will draw moisture out of the meat over time, making the meat tastier, yes, but also drier. So how long should you use a rub? Here are some guidelines.

UP TO 15 MINUTES:	cubed meat for kabobs
15 TO 30 MINUTES:	boneless chicken breasts
30 MINUTES TO 1½ HOURS:	bone-in chicken pieces and whole chickens
2 TO 8 HOURS:	turkey

A WORD ABOUT FRESHNESS

Ground spices lose their aromas in a matter of months (eight to ten months maximum). If you have been holding onto a little jar of coriander for years, waiting to blend the world's finest version of curry powder, forget about it. Dump the old, tired coriander and buy some freshly ground. Better yet, but whole coriander and grind the seeds yourself. Some people who are far more exacting than I am actually date each jar when they buy it. Whatever you do, store your spices in airtight containers away from light and heat, to give them a long, aromatic life.

RUB RECIPES FOR CHICKEN

Chicken Rub
MAKES: about ⅓ cup

- 4 teaspoons granulated onion
- 4 teaspoons granulated garlic
- 1 tablespoon kosher salt
- 2 teaspoons prepared chili powder
- 2 teaspoons ground black pepper

Magic Rub
MAKES: 2 tablespoons

- 1 teaspoon dry mustard
- 1 teaspoon granulated onion
- 1 teaspoon paprika
- 1 teaspoon kosher salt
- ½ teaspoon granulated garlic
- ½ teaspoon ground coriander
- ½ teaspoon ground cumin
- ½ teaspoon ground black pepper

Cajun Rub
MAKES: about 3 tablespoons

- 2 teaspoons finely chopped fresh thyme leaves
- 1½ teaspoons kosher salt
- 1 teaspoon granulated garlic
- 1 teaspoon granulated onion
- 1 teaspoon paprika
- 1 teaspoon light brown sugar
- ¾ teaspoon ground black pepper
- ¼ teaspoon ground cayenne pepper

Fennel Rub
MAKES: ¼ cup

- 1 tablespoon ground fennel seed
- 1 tablespoon kosher salt
- 1 tablespoon pure chile powder
- 1½ teaspoons celery seed
- 1½ teaspoons ground black pepper

Barbecue Chicken Rub
MAKES: about 3 tablespoons

- 1 tablespoon smoked paprika
- 2 teaspoons dry mustard
- 1 teaspoon kosher salt
- ½ teaspoon granulated garlic
- ½ teaspoon granulated onion
- ¼ teaspoon chipotle chile powder

All-Purpose Rub
MAKES: about 2 tablespoons

- 1 teaspoon pure chile powder
- 1 teaspoon granulated garlic
- 1 teaspoon paprika
- 1 teaspoon kosher salt
- ½ teaspoon ground coriander
- ½ teaspoon ground cumin
- ½ teaspoon ground black pepper

New World Rub
MAKES: about 2 tablespoons

- 1 teaspoon granulated garlic
- 1 teaspoon granulated onion
- 1 teaspoon paprika
- ½ teaspoon ground cumin
- ½ teaspoon dried lemongrass
- ½ teaspoon dried basil
- ½ teaspoon dried thyme
- ½ teaspoon kosher salt
- ¼ teaspoon ground black pepper

Lemon-Paprika Rub
MAKES: about 2 tablespoons

- 2 teaspoons smoked paprika
- 2 teaspoons kosher salt
- Finely grated zest of 1 lemon
- ½ teaspoon granulated garlic
- ½ teaspoon ground black pepper

Marinades

Marinades work more slowly than rubs, but they can seep in a little deeper. Typically a marinade is made with some acidic liquid, some oil, and some combination of herbs and spices. These ingredients can fill in the gaps when a particular cut of meat lacks enough taste or richness. They can also give food characteristics that reflect regional and ethnic cooking styles.

HOW LONG SHOULD I MARINATE?

The right times vary depending on the strength of the marinade and the food you are marinating. If your marinade includes intense ingredients, such as soy sauce, liquor, or hot chiles and spices, don't overdo it. If an acidic marinade is left too long on meat, it can make the surface mushy or dry. Here are some general guidelines to get you going.

15 TO 30 MINUTES:	cubed chicken for kabobs
1 TO 3 HOURS:	boneless chicken breasts
2 TO 6 HOURS:	bone-in chicken pieces and whole chickens
6 TO 12 HOURS:	turkey

NOTE

Marinades work faster at room temperature, but if the food requires more than 30 minutes of marinating time, put it in the refrigerator.

TIPS

When the marinade includes an acid, be sure to use non-reactive containers. These are dishes made of glass, plastic, stainless steel, or ceramic. Containers made of aluminum or metals other than stainless steel react with acids and add a metallic flavor to food. My favorite container is a resealable plastic bag. I set the bag in a bowl so the liquid comes up the sides of the food and covers it evenly. If there is not enough liquid, I turn the bag over every so often.

After a marinade has been in contact with raw meat, either discard it or boil it for at least 1 minute. The boiling will destroy any harmful bacteria that might have been left by the meat. A boiled marinade often works well as a basting sauce, too.

MARINADE RECIPES FOR CHICKEN

Teriyaki Marinade
MAKES: about 2 cups

1 cup pineapple juice
½ cup low-sodium soy sauce
½ cup finely chopped yellow onion
1 tablespoon toasted sesame oil
1 tablespoon grated fresh ginger
1 tablespoon minced garlic
1 tablespoon dark brown sugar
1 tablespoon fresh lemon juice

Jerk Marinade
MAKES: about ¾ cup

½ cup roughly chopped yellow onion
1 jalapeño chile pepper, roughly chopped
3 tablespoons white wine vinegar
2 tablespoons soy sauce
2 tablespoons canola oil
½ teaspoon ground allspice
¼ teaspoon granulated garlic
¼ teaspoon ground cinnamon
¼ teaspoon kosher salt
¼ teaspoon ground black pepper
⅛ teaspoon ground nutmeg

1. In a food processor combine the ingredients and process until smooth.

Pacific Rim Marinade
MAKES: about 1 cup

¼ cup ketchup
¼ cup hoisin sauce
2 tablespoons rice vinegar
2 tablespoons soy sauce
4 teaspoons curry powder
4 teaspoons toasted sesame oil
¼ teaspoon Tabasco® sauce

Tequila Marinade
MAKES: about 1¾ cups

1 cup fresh orange juice
½ cup tequila
2 tablespoons fresh lime juice
2 tablespoons light brown sugar
2 teaspoons ground cumin
1 jalapeño chile pepper, finely chopped

Mojo Marinade
MAKES: about ¾ cup

¼ cup fresh orange juice
3 tablespoons fresh lime juice
3 tablespoons extra-virgin olive oil
2 tablespoons finely chopped fresh cilantro leaves
1 tablespoon finely chopped jalapeño chile pepper
1 tablespoon minced garlic
¾ teaspoon ground cumin
½ teaspoon kosher salt

Marinades

Lemon-Sage Marinade
MAKES: about 1 cup

 1 tablespoon grated lemon zest
 ¼ cup fresh lemon juice
 ¼ cup extra-virgin olive oil
 3 tablespoons finely chopped fresh sage leaves
 2 tablespoons minced shallot
 2 tablespoons whole-grain mustard
 1 tablespoon finely chopped garlic
 1 tablespoon cracked black peppercorns

Beer Marinade
MAKES: about 1¼ cups

 1 cup dark Mexican beer
 2 tablespoons toasted sesame oil
 1 tablespoon finely chopped garlic
 1 teaspoon dried oregano
 1 teaspoon kosher salt
 ½ teaspoon ground black pepper
 ¼ teaspoon ground cayenne pepper

Greek Marinade
MAKES: about ½ cup

 6 tablespoons extra-virgin olive oil
 3 tablespoons red wine vinegar
 ½ teaspoon minced garlic
 ½ teaspoon kosher salt
 ½ teaspoon dried oregano
 ¼ teaspoon crushed red pepper flakes

Honey-Mustard Marinade
MAKES: about 1 cup

 ½ cup Dijon mustard
 ¼ cup honey
 2 tablespoons extra-virgin olive oil
 2 teaspoons curry powder
 1 teaspoon grated lemon zest
 ½ teaspoon granulated garlic
 ½ teaspoon kosher salt
 ¼ teaspoon ground cayenne pepper
 ¼ teaspoon ground black pepper

Mango Marinade
MAKES: about 1½ cups

 1 cup mango juice
 ¼ cup rice vinegar
 3 tablespoons extra-virgin olive oil
 2 tablespoons soy sauce
 2 tablespoons minced shallot
 2 teaspoons minced garlic
 2 teaspoons hot chili-garlic sauce, such as Sriracha
 1 teaspoon kosher salt
 ½ teaspoon ground cumin
 ½ teaspoon ground black pepper

NOTE!
You can substitute apricot or orange juice for the mango juice, if desired.

130

Sauces

Sauces open up a world of flavors for grillers. They offer us almost limitless ways for distinguishing our food and making it more interesting. Once you have learned some of the fundamentals about balancing flavors and some of the techniques for holding sauces together, you are ready to develop your own. The next couple of pages provide some tasty examples of sauces that work particularly well with chicken.

SAUCE RECIPES FOR CHICKEN

Pasilla Barbecue Sauce
MAKES: about 2 cups

- 2 tablespoons extra-virgin olive oil
- 6 medium garlic cloves, peeled
- ⅓ cup finely chopped red onion
- 2 dried pasilla chile peppers, stemmed, seeded, and cut into strips
- 1 cup diced canned tomatoes with juice
- 1 cup amber Mexican beer
- 1 tablespoon cider vinegar
- 1 teaspoon kosher salt
- ½ teaspoon dried oregano
- ¼ teaspoon ground black pepper

1. In a small, heavy-bottomed saucepan over medium heat, warm the oil and cook the garlic until lightly browned, 4 to 5 minutes, turning occasionally. Add the onion and chiles. Cook for about 3 minutes, stirring occasionally. Add the remaining ingredients, bring to a boil, and then simmer for 15 minutes. Remove the saucepan from the heat and let the mixture stand for 15 minutes to soften the chiles and blend the flavors. Puree in a blender.

Rémoulade
MAKES: about ¾ cup

- ½ cup mayonnaise
- 1 tablespoon capers, drained and minced
- 1 tablespoon sweet pickle relish
- 1 tablespoon finely chopped fresh tarragon leaves
- 2 teaspoons minced shallot
- 1 teaspoon tarragon vinegar
- 1 teaspoon minced garlic
- ½ teaspoon Dijon mustard
- ¼ teaspoon paprika
- ⅛ teaspoon kosher salt

1. In a medium glass or stainless steel bowl, whisk the ingredients. If not using right away, cover and refrigerate for as long as 24 hours.

Tomato Salsa
MAKES: about 2 cups

- 1½ cups finely diced ripe tomatoes
- ½ cup finely diced white onion, rinsed in a sieve under cold water
- 2 tablespoons finely chopped fresh cilantro leaves
- 1 tablespoon extra-virgin olive oil
- 2 teaspoons fresh lime juice
- 1 teaspoon minced jalapeño chile pepper, with seeds
- ¼ teaspoon dried oregano
- ¼ teaspoon kosher salt
- ¼ teaspoon ground black pepper

1. In a medium glass or stainless steel bowl, mix the ingredients. If desired, to fully incorporate the flavors, let the salsa sit at room temperature for about 1 hour. Drain in a sieve just before serving.

Sauces

Roasted Tomatillo Salsa
MAKES: about 1 cup

- 1 small yellow onion, cut crosswise into ½-inch slices
- Extra-virgin olive oil
- 8 medium tomatillos, about 8 ounces total, husked and rinsed
- 1 medium poblano chile pepper
- ¼ cup loosely packed fresh cilantro leaves and tender stems
- 1 medium garlic clove, crushed
- ½ teaspoon dark brown sugar
- ½ teaspoon kosher salt

1. Prepare the grill for direct cooking over high heat (450° to 550°F).

2. Lightly brush the onion slices on both sides with oil. Grill the onions, tomatillos, and chile over ***direct high heat***, with the lid closed as much as possible, until lightly charred all over, 6 to 8 minutes, turning once or twice. Transfer the onion and tomatillos to a blender or food processor and place the chile on a work surface. When the chile is cool enough to handle, remove and discard the skin, stem, and seeds. Add the chile to the blender along with the remaining ingredients. Process until fairly smooth. Taste and adjust the seasonings, if necessary.

Classic Red Barbecue Sauce
MAKES: about 1¼ cups

- ¾ cup apple juice
- ¼ cup ketchup
- 3 tablespoons cider vinegar
- 2 teaspoons soy sauce
- 1 teaspoon Worcestershire sauce
- 1 teaspoon molasses
- ½ teaspoon pure chile powder
- ½ teaspoon granulated garlic
- ¼ teaspoon ground black pepper

1. In a small saucepan mix the ingredients. Simmer for a few minutes over medium heat, and then remove the saucepan from the heat.

Sassy Barbecue Sauce
MAKES: about 1 cup

- ½ cup water
- ½ cup ketchup
- 2 tablespoons molasses
- 1 tablespoon white wine vinegar
- 1 tablespoon Dijon mustard
- 1 tablespoon light brown sugar
- 2 teaspoons Worcestershire sauce
- ½ teaspoon kosher salt
- ¼ teaspoon Tabasco® sauce
- ¼ teaspoon granulated garlic
- ¼ teaspoon ground black pepper

1. In a small, heavy-bottomed saucepan whisk the ingredients. Bring to boil over medium heat, then reduce the heat and simmer for 10 minutes, stirring occasionally.

Balinese Peanut Sauce
MAKES: about 1¼ cups

½ cup smooth peanut butter
½ cup stirred unsweetened coconut milk
2 tablespoons fresh lime juice
2 teaspoons hot chili-garlic sauce, such as Sriracha
2 teaspoons fish sauce

1. In a small saucepan combine the ingredients. Set the saucepan over very low heat and cook until the sauce is smooth, 3 to 5 minutes, whisking occasionally, but do not let the sauce simmer. If the sauce seems too thick, whisk in 1 to 2 tablespoons of water.

Chimichurri Sauce
MAKES: about 1½ cups

4 large garlic cloves
1 cup loosely packed fresh Italian parsley leaves and tender stems
1 cup loosely packed fresh cilantro leaves
½ cup loosely packed fresh basil leaves
¾ cup extra-virgin olive oil
¼ cup rice vinegar
1 teaspoon kosher salt
½ teaspoon ground black pepper
½ teaspoon Tabasco® sauce

1. In a food processor with the motor running, mince the garlic. Add the parsley, cilantro, and basil. Pulse to finely chop the herbs. With the motor running, slowly add the oil in a thin stream, and then add the remaining ingredients.

Romesco Sauce
MAKES: about ¾ cup

2 medium red bell peppers
1 medium garlic clove
¼ cup whole almonds, toasted
½ cup loosely packed fresh Italian parsley leaves
2 teaspoons sherry vinegar
½ teaspoon kosher salt
⅛ teaspoon ground cayenne pepper
¼ cup extra-virgin olive oil

1. Prepare the grill for direct cooking over medium heat (350° to 450°F).

2. Grill the bell peppers over *direct medium heat*, with the lid closed as much as possible, until they are blackened and blistered all over, 12 to 15 minutes, turning occasionally. Place the peppers in a small bowl and cover with plastic wrap. Set aside for about 10 minutes, then remove and discard the skins, stems, and seeds.

3. In a food processor finely chop the garlic. Add the almonds and process until finely chopped. Add the peppers, parsley, vinegar, salt, and cayenne. Process to create a coarse paste. With the motor running, slowly add the oil and process until you have a fairly smooth sauce.

Grilling Guide for Chicken

The following cuts, weights, and grilling times are meant to be guidelines rather than hard and fast rules. Cooking times are affected by such factors as altitude, wind, and outside temperature. Grill boneless chicken pieces using the direct method for the time given on the chart, turning once or twice. Grill whole chickens using the indirect method, and bone-in chicken pieces using both direct and indirect methods for the time given on the chart, or until an instant-read thermometer reaches the desired doneness. Cooking times are for the USDA's recommendation of 170°F for breast meat and 180°F for thigh meat. Let whole chickens rest for 5 to 10 minutes before carving. The internal temperature of the meat will rise by 5 to 10 degrees during this time.

CHICKEN	WEIGHT	APPROXIMATE GRILLING TIME
Chicken breast, boneless, skinless	6 to 8 ounces	**8 to 12 minutes** direct medium heat
Chicken thigh, boneless, skinless	4 ounces	**8 to 10 minutes** direct medium heat
Chicken breast, bone-in	10 to 12 ounces	**23 to 35 minutes:** 3 to 5 minutes direct medium heat, 20 to 30 minutes indirect medium heat
Chicken thigh, bone-in	5 to 6 ounces	**36 to 40 minutes:** 6 to 10 minutes direct medium heat, 30 minutes indirect medium heat
Chicken drumstick	3 to 4 ounces	**36 to 40 minutes:** 6 to 10 minutes direct medium heat, 30 minutes indirect medium heat
Chicken, whole leg	10 to 12 ounces	**48 minutes to 1 hour:** 8 to 10 minutes direct medium heat, 40 to 50 minutes indirect medium heat
Chicken wing	2 to 3 ounces	**35 to 43 minutes:** 5 to 8 minutes direct medium heat, 30 to 35 minutes indirect medium heat
Chicken, whole	4 to 5 pounds	**1 to 1¼ hours** indirect medium heat
Ground chicken thigh meat	¾ inch thick	**12 to 14 minutes** direct medium heat

HOW TO CUT UP A WHOLE CHICKEN

Cut the twine and remove it. With the breast side facing up, cut through the skin between the first leg and the breast.

Once you have cut through the skin, pull the leg away from the breast and bend it behind the chicken. The joint that holds the leg to the chicken will pop up.

Cut through the joint to remove the leg. Repeat the process with the second leg.

Lift each wing to expose the joint that connects it to the chicken. Cut through each joint to remove the wings.

Cut along either side of the breastbone. Work the knife over the top of the rib cage on either side of the breastbone, and push the meat away from the bones.

Cut through the joint between each thigh and drumstick.

GRILL WHAT'S GROWING AT THE TIME

Vegetables in season locally have big advantages over whatever has been shipped from across the world. They are riper, so they taste better. That means you can grill them simply with great results.

EXPOSE AS MUCH SURFACE AREA AS POSSIBLE

Cut each vegetable to give you the biggest area to put in direct contact with the cooking grates. The more direct contact, the better the flavors will be. For example, choose peppers with flat sides that you can easily slice off the core. The flatter the sides, the more surface area will caramelize on the hot cooking grates.

USE THE GOOD OIL

Vegetables need oil to prevent sticking and burning. Neutral oils like canola oil will do the job fine, but an extra-virgin olive oil provides the added benefit of improving the flavor of virtually every vegetable. Brush on just enough to coat each side thoroughly but not so much that the vegetables would drip oil and cause flare-ups. Season the vegetables generously with salt and pepper (some of it will fall off). For more flavors, marinate the vegetables at room temperature for 20 minutes to an hour in olive oil, vinegar, garlic, herbs, and spices.

WHEN IS IT DONE?

I like firm vegetables such as onions and fennel to be somewhere between crisp and tender. If you want them softer, grill them a few minutes longer, although watch them carefully for burning. The grill intensifies the sweetness of vegetables quickly and that can lead to burning. Cut the vegetables as evenly as you can. A ½-inch thickness is right for most of them.

Just about everything from artichokes to zucchini tends to cook best over direct medium heat. The temperature on the grill's thermometer should be somewhere between 350° and 450°F. If any parts get a little too dark, turn the vegetables over. Otherwise turn them as few times as possible.

VEGETABLES	THICKNESS/SIZE	APPROXIMATE GRILLING TIME
Artichoke (10 to 12 ounces)	whole	**14 to 18 minutes:** boil 10 to 12 minutes; cut in half and grill 4 to 6 minutes direct medium heat
Asparagus	½-inch diameter	**6 to 8 minutes** direct medium heat
Bell pepper	whole	**10 to 15 minutes** direct medium heat
Bell/Chile pepper	¼-inch slices	**6 to 8 minutes** direct medium heat
Carrot	1-inch diameter	**7 to 11 minutes:** boil 4 to 6 minutes, grill 3 to 5 minutes direct high heat
Corn, husked		**10 to 15 minutes** direct medium heat
Corn, in husk		**25 to 30 minutes** direct medium heat
Eggplant	½-inch slices	**8 to 10 minutes** direct medium heat
Fennel	¼-inch slices	**10 to 12 minutes** direct medium heat
Garlic	whole	**45 minutes to 1 hour** indirect medium heat
Mushroom, shiitake or button		**8 to 10 minutes** direct medium heat
Mushroom, portabello		**10 to 15 minutes** direct medium heat
Onion	halved	**35 to 40 minutes** indirect medium heat
	½-inch slices	**8 to 12 minutes** direct medium heat
Potato	whole	**45 minutes to 1 hour** indirect medium heat
	½-inch slices	**14 to 16 minutes** direct medium heat
Potato, new	halved	**15 to 20 minutes** direct medium heat
Scallion	whole	**3 to 4 minutes** direct medium heat
Squash, acorn	1½ pounds, halved	**40 minutes to 1 hour** indirect medium heat
Sweet potato	whole	**50 minutes to 1 hour** indirect medium heat
	¼-inch slices	**8 to 10 minutes** direct medium heat
Tomato, garden or plum	halved	**6 to 8 minutes** direct medium heat
	whole	**8 to 10 minutes** direct medium heat
Zucchini	½-inch slices	**3 to 5 minutes** direct medium heat
	halved	**4 to 6 minutes** direct medium heat

Safety

Please read your owner's guide and familiarize yourself with and follow all "dangers," "warnings," and "cautions." Also follow the grilling procedures and maintenance requirements contained in your owner's guide. If you cannot locate the owner's guide for your grill model, please contact the manufacturer prior to use.

If you have any questions concerning the "dangers," "warnings," and "cautions" contained in your Weber® gas or charcoal owner's guide, or if you do not have an owner's guide for your specific grill model, please contact Weber-Stephen Products Co. Customer Service at 1.800.446.1071 before using your grill. You can also access your owner's guide online at www.weber.com.

GENERAL NOTES

1. Grills radiate a lot of heat, so always keep the grill at least five feet away from any combustible materials, including the house, garage, deck rails, etc. Combustible materials include, but are not limited to, wood or treated wood decks, wood patios, or wood porches. Never use a grill indoors or under a covered patio.

2. Keep the grill in a level position at all times.

3. Use proper barbecuing tools with long, heat-resistant handles.

4. Don't wear loose or highly flammable clothing when grilling.

5. Do not leave infants, children, or pets unattended near a hot grill.

6. Use barbecue mitts to protect hands while cooking or adjusting the vents.

GAS GRILL SAFETY

1. Always keep the bottom tray and grease catch pan of your gas grill clean and free of debris. This not only prevents dangerous grease fires, it deters visits from unwanted critters.

2. If a flare-up should occur, make sure the lid is closed. Then, if necessary, move the food over indirect heat until the flare-up subsides. Never use water to extinguish flames on a gas grill.

3. Do not line the funnel-shaped bottom tray with foil. This could prevent grease from flowing into the grease catch pan. Grease is also likely to catch in the tiny creases of the foil and start a fire.

4. Never store propane tanks or spares indoors (that means the garage, too).

5. For the first few uses, the temperature of a new gas grill may run hotter than normal. Once your grill is seasoned and the inside of the cooking box is less reflective, the temperature will return to normal.

CHARCOAL GRILL SAFETY

1. Charcoal grills are designed for outdoor use only. If used indoors, toxic fumes will accumulate and cause serious bodily injury or death.

2. Do not add charcoal starter fluid or charcoal impregnated with charcoal starter fluid to hot or warm charcoal.

3. Do not use gasoline, alcohol, or other highly volatile fluids to ignite charcoal. If using charcoal starter fluid, remove any fluid that may have drained through the bottom vents before lighting the charcoal.

4. Do not use a grill unless all parts are in place. Make sure the ash catcher is properly attached to the legs underneath the bowl of the grill.

5. Remove the lid from the grill while lighting and getting the charcoal started.

6. Always put charcoal on top of the charcoal grate, not into the bottom of the bowl.

7. Do not place a chimney starter on or near any combustible surface.

8. Never touch the cooking or charcoal grate or the grill to see if it is hot.

9. Use the hook on the inside of the lid to hang the lid on the side of the bowl of the grill. Avoid placing a hot lid on carpet or grass. Do not hang the lid on the bowl handle.

10. To extinguish the coals, place the lid on the bowl and close all of the vents (dampers). Make sure that the vents on the lid and the bowl are completely closed. Do not use water, as it will damage the porcelain finish.

11. If a flare-up should occur, place the lid on the grill and close the top vent about halfway. If the flames are still threatening, open the lid and move the food over indirect heat. Do not use water to extinguish the flames.

12. Handle and store hot electric starters carefully. Do not place starters on or near any combustible surfaces.

13. Keep electrical cords away from the hot surfaces of the grill.

Index

Index

142

Index